GH00514690

THE TOP 11 OF EVERYTHING RED

Liverpool

IT'S NOT TRIVIA, IT'S MORE IMPORTANT THAN THAT

Written by
Chris Hughes

Text editors Paul Simpson,
Helen Rodiss, Michaela Bushell

Production
Ian Cranna, Tim Harrison,
Tim Oldham, Andy Pringle

Cover and book design
Sharon O'Connor

Cover image Plain
Picture/Photolibrary

Thanks to
Mark Ellingham, Simon Kanter,
Andrew Lockett, Nick, Steph,
Dave, John, Bernie, Dan, Ryan
and Jim for the good times on
the road to Istanbul. Special
thanks to Ian Jones for the
repeated loan of his sofa

Printed in Spain
by Graphy Cems

This edition published
July 2005 was prepared by
Haymarket Network for
Rough Guides Ltd,
80 Strand, London, WC2R ORL

Distributed by the
Penguin Group
Penguin Books Ltd,
27 Wrights Lane,
London W8 5TZ

A catalogue record for this
book is available from the
British Library

ISBN 1-84353-563-7

Contents

ABSOLUTE BEST MOMENTS

113 years of glorious history on the back of a postage stamp

1. Six miraculous minutes – or why do things the easy way? May 2005
Maldini puts Milan in front. Two from Crespo and we're down and out. But a half-time blast of YNWA is the prelude for six magical minutes – a Gerrard header, a rifle-shot from Smicer and Xabi Alonso's penalty rebound pull Liverpool level. Taking the game to penalties, Dudek's dancing means the European Cup returns to Anfield. Forever.

2. Allez les Rouges May 1977
Liverpool were heading out of the 1977 European Cup on away goals at the hands of the French champions St Etienne with six minutes left on the clock, until scrawny substitute David Fairclough slotted home after a through-ball from Ray Kennedy. The ground literally trembled with the noise and relief of 55,043 fans.

3. The Double May 1986
It had looked impossible back in February after Everton had established a decisive lead in the title race, but the Reds crept up on the rails, overtaking the Blues and securing the league on the last day at Stamford Bridge with a Dalglish classic, before beating Everton again at Wembley to win the third Double of the 20th century.

4. Ian St John wins the Cup May 1965
They said the Liver Birds would fly off down the Mersey if Liverpool ever won the FA Cup, but after 73 years of heartbreak and failure, Ian St John finally brought the trophy back to Merseyside, his diving header in extra time converting Ian Callaghan's floated cross. The Liver Birds are still there.

5. The Hillsborough Cup final May 1989
One month after 96 Liverpool supporters had lost their lives watching the semi-final at Hillsborough, the Reds lifted the FA Cup on an emotional afternoon at Wembley. Gerry sang *You'll Never Walk Alone*, Aldridge scored with practically his first touch, Stuart McCall equalised twice for Everton but substitute Ian Rush had the final say.

6. Ian Rush scores four 6 November 1982
This afternoon the incredible Mr Rush etched himself into the history books by becoming the first player in 47 years to score four goals in a Merseyside derby, demolishing his boyhood heroes at Goodison Park with a matchless exhibition of finishing.

7. Pass and move May 1974
In 1974, Liverpool tore Newcastle United apart at Wembley, stripped them naked even, as David Coleman put it, playing exhibition pass-and-move football. It almost seemed like Shankly was conducting his orchestral team from the touchline like a maestro, intuitively anticipating every ball and run.

8. Shankly addresses the multitudes May 1971
Liverpool had lost the 1971 FA Cup final to Arsenal but half a million supporters still turned out to greet them on their return to Merseyside. As Bill Shankly declared on surveying the throng from the balcony of St George's Hall: "Even Chairman Mao has never seen a greater display of red strength."

9. Better than the Brazilians April 1988
The football played by the 1987/88 team of John Barnes, Peter Beardsley, John Aldridge et al remains the most entertaining seen in the English game, the apex being a 5-0 drubbing of Nottingham Forest on a Wednesday night at Anfield. Tom Finney, watching from the stands, reckoned it was the best footballing exhibition he'd ever seen, even better than Brazil.

> TOM FINNEY RECKONED IT WAS THE BEST FOOTBALL HE'D EVER SEEN – EVEN BETTER THAN THE BRAZILIANS

10. Houllier's return March 2002
On 13 October 2001, Gerard Houllier had been taken to hospital for heart surgery during a game against Leeds United. Five months later, he made an emotional return for a Champions League decider against Roma. Fabio Capello embraced him and Jari Litmanen and Emile Heskey grabbed the two goals for Liverpool to go through.

11. Liverpool 4 Newcastle 3 April 1996
Robbie Fowler put the Reds in front, Les Ferdinand equalised for Keegan's title contenders, David Ginola gave them the lead, Fowler levelled it, Faustino Asprilla put Newcastle back in front and celebrated in front of the Liverpool fans. Stan Collymore made it 3-3 before settling it in the last pulsating minute of one extraordinary night.

ALL-TIME MOST APPEARANCES

The first names on the teamsheet, week in, week out

1. **Ian Callaghan** 856
2. **Ray Clemence** 666
3. **Emlyn Hughes** 665
4. **Ian Rush** 658
5. **Phil Neal** 648
6. **Tommy Smith** 637
7. **Bruce Grobbelaar** 627
8. **Alan Hansen** 623
9. **Chris Lawler** 549
10. **Billy Liddell** 537
11. **Kenny Dalglish** 511

ALL-TIME TOP GOALSCORERS

The peerless predators who rewrote the Red record books

1. **Ian Rush** 346
2. **Roger Hunt** 286
3. **Gordon Hodgson** 240
4. **Billy Liddell** 229
5. **Kenny Dalglish** 172
6. **Robbie Fowler** 171
7. **Michael Owen** 158
8. **Harry Chambers** 151
9. **Jack Parkinson** 128
10. **Sam Raybould** 127
11. **Dick Forshaw** 124

ALMOST REDS

From Law to Laudrup, the men who almost entered Anfield folklore

1. Denis Law
One of the first things Bill Shankly did as Liverpool manager was attempt to sign the lethal Scot he'd blooded as a 16-year-old at Huddersfield. But the Anfield board

refused to sanction the transfer and the striker joined Manchester City the following year. Five years later, Law had become European Footballer of the Year.

2. Jack Charlton

In his first season as boss, Shankly also made an £18,000 bid for the lanky defender, then languishing at the bottom of the table with Leeds United. But the Elland Road club decided Liverpool's valuation was too low, so the Reds signed Ron Yeats instead.

3. Frank Worthington

The flamboyant Elvis fan actually signed a Liverpool contract during the 1971/72 season, but his blood pressure was deemed too high by the club doctor. The Leicester striker was packed off on holiday, but on his return his pressure was even higher. Rumours have surrounded the breakdown of the deal for three decades.

4. Lou Macari

In 1973, Shankly invited the prolific Celtic striker to Anfield to watch a game and tabled a £200,000 bid. But the Scot decided to accept an offer from Manchester United, leaving Shanks to fume: "I only wanted him for the reserves anyway!"

5. Charlie Nicholas

The Celtic striker had the chance to join Liverpool in 1983 but opted for Arsenal. Dalglish later admitted he'd have loved to play alongside Charlie but suggested Nicholas feared he might not make the team. It's rumoured that Liverpool withdrew their bid because Nicholas arrived for contract talks in a colourful leather suit.

6. Michael Laudrup

Like most leading European clubs in the spring of 1983, Liverpool were desperate to get their hands on the 17-year-old Danish wunderkind. Tom Saunders was despatched to Denmark for negotiations, but the deal foundered on the length of the contract. Laudrup eventually signed for Juventus.

7. Ian Snodin

Things got a bit heated around the start of 1987 as Liverpool and Everton battled for the signature of the Leeds United captain. Kenny Dalglish had already agreed personal terms with the midfielder when Howard Kendall made an 11th-hour bid and lured him across Stanley Park to Dalglish's public irritation.

8. Paul Gascoigne

On signing for Tottenham from Newcastle in the summer of 1988, it's rumoured Gazza attempted to get a clause inserted into his contract stating that if Liverpool were to ever bid for him, he would be free to move to Anfield. Not surprisingly, Spurs manager Terry Venables rapidly put an end to that idea.

9. Eric Cantona
Graeme Souness has revealed that he was offered the chance to sign the mercurial Frenchman in the early1990s. "At that time we didn't really need any more problems, so that was one that got away," said Souness of the player who scored 88 goals for Manchester United and inspired them to four Premiership titles.

10. Luis Figo
In 1995, Roy Evans tabled a £1.4m bid to sign the future Portuguese superstar from Sporting Lisbon, but Barcelona topped Liverpool's bid.

11. Rivaldo
"If I could choose my next team, and if they want me, it will be Liverpool," declared the Brazilian ace in 2003. "It would be an honour for me to wear their red shirt and I would regard it as a dream to play alongside Michael Owen." Gerard Houllier didn't take him up on his offer, believing the 31-year-old was too great a financial risk.

ANFIELD ANTHEMS
Some old, some new, all sung with pride and passion

1. The Fields Of Anfield Road
Outside the Shankly Gates/heard a Kopite calling/Shankly they have taken you away/But you left a great 11/Before you went to heaven/Now it's glory round the fields of Anfield Road

All round the fields of Anfield Road/Where once we watched the King Kenny play (and could he play)/We had Heighway on the wing/We had dreams and songs to sing/Of the glory round the fields of Anfield Road

Outside the Paisley Gates/I heard a Kopite calling/Paisley they have taken you away/You led the great eleven/Back in Rome in 77/And the Redmen, they're still playing the same way

2. Poor Scouser Tommy
Let me tell you the story of a poor boy/Who was sent far away from his home/To fight for his king and his country/And also the old folks back home/So they put him in a Highland

division/Sent him off to a far foreign land/Where the flies swarm around in their thousands/And there's nothing to see but the sand

The battle it started next morning/Under the Arabian sun/I remember that poor Scouser Tommy/He was shot by an old Nazi gun/As he lay on the battle field dying (dying dying)/With the blood gushing out of his head (of his head)/As he lay on the battle field dying (dying dying)/These were the last words he said…

> "SHANKLY IS OUR HERO HE SHOWED US HOW TO PLAY, THE MIGHTY REDS OF EUROPE ARE OUT TO WIN TODAY"

Oh, I am a Liverpudlian/I come from the Spion Kop/I like to sing, I like to shout/I go there quite a lot (every week)/We support a team that's dressed in red/It's a team that you all know/It's a team that we call Liverpool/And to glory we will go

We've won the League, we've won the Cup/We've been to Europe too/We played the Toffees for a laugh/And we left them feeling blue (five-nil!)

One two/One two three/One two three four/Five-nil!/Rush scored one/Rush scored two/Rush scored three and Rush scored four/La la la, la la, la la

3. We All Live In A Red And White Kop
On a Saturday afternoon/We support a team called Liverpool /And we sing until we drop/On the famous Spion Kop/We all live in a red and white Kop/A red and white Kop/A red and white Kop/We all live in a red and white Kop/A red and white Kop/A red and white Kop

4. The Reds Are Coming Up The Hill
The Reds are coming up the hill, boys/The Reds are coming up the hill/They all laugh at us/They all mock us/They all say our days are numbered/Born to be a Scouse/Victoriously/If you wanna win the cup /Then you better hurry up/Cos we're Liverpool FC /Victorious and glorious/We took the Gwladys Street between the four of us /So you better thank God there was only f***ing four/Imagine what we'd done if there was more of us.

5. A Liver Bird Upon My Chest
Here's a song about a football team/The greatest team you've ever seen/A team that play total football/They've won the league, Europe and all

A Liver Bird upon my chest/We are the men of Shankly's best/A team that plays the

Liverpool way/And wins the championship in May

With Kenny Dalglish on the ball /He was the greatest of them all/And Ian Rush, four goals or two/Left Evertonians feeling blue

Now if you go down Goodison way/Hard luck stories you hear each day/There's not a trophy to be seen/Cos Liverpool have swept them clean

Now on the glorious tenth of May/There's laughing reds on Wembley Way/We're full of smiles and joy and glee/It's Everton 1 and Liverpool 3

Now on the 20th of May/We're laughing still on Wembley Way/Those Evertonians feeling blue/At Liverpool 3 and Everton 2

And as we sang round Goodison Park/With crying Blues all in a nark/They're probably crying still/At Liverpool 5 and Everton nil

We remember them with pride/Those mighty Reds of Shankly's side/And Kenny's boys of 88/ There's never been a side so great

Now back in 1965/When great Bill Shankly was alive/We're playing Leeds, the score's 1-1/When it fell to the head of Ian St John

On April 15th 89/What should have been a joyous time/Ninety-six friends, we all shall miss/And all the Kopites want justice

6. Liverpool We Love You

We love you Liverpool we do/We love you Liverpool we do/We love you Liverpool we do/ We love you Liverpool we do/Oh Liverpool we love you

Shankly is our hero, he showed us how to play/The mighty Reds of Europe are out to win today/He made a team of champions, with every man a king/And every game we love to win and this is what we sing

Clemence is our goalie, the best there is around/And Keegan is the greatest that Shankly ever found/Heighway is our favourite, a wizard of the game/And here's the mighty Toshack to do it once again

We've won the league, we've won the cup, we're masters of the game/And just to prove how good we are, we'll do it all again/We've got another team to beat and so we've got to try/'Cos we're the best in all the land and that's the reason why

7. We Hate Nottingham Forest
We hate Nottingham Forest/We hate Everton too (they're shit!)/We hate Man United But Liverpool we love you (all together now)

8. Men Of Anfield
Stevie Heighway's always running/John Toshack is always scoring/Then you'll hear the Kopites roaring/Toshack is our king/Men of Anfield here's our story/We have gone from great to glory/We're the greatest team in Europe/Toshack is our king!

9. When The Reds Go Marching In
Oh when the Reds/Go marching in/Oh when the Reds go marching in/I want to be in that number/When the Reds go marching in

10. The Best Behaved Supporters In The Land
We're the best behaved supporters in the land (when we win)/We're the best behaved supporters in the land (when we win)/We're the best behaved supporters/The best behaved supporters/We're the best behaved supporters in the land (when we win)

We're a right shower of bastards when we lose / We're a right shower of bastards when we lose / We're a right shower of bastards/A right shower of bastards when we lose/ We're a right shower of bastards when we lose (but we don't)

11. L-I-V-E-R-P-O-O-L
L-I-V / E-R-P / Double O, L/Liverpool FC!

BATTLES OF BRITAIN (AND IRELAND)

11 European ties against British teams

1. **Liverpool 2 Celtic 1** Cup Winners' Cup, semi-final, 1965/66
2. **Liverpool 14 Dundalk 0** Inter-Cities Fairs Cup, first round, 1969/70
3. **Liverpool 3 Hibernian 0** Inter-Cities Fairs Cup, third round, 1970/71
4. **Liverpool 0 Leeds United 1** Inter-Cities Fairs Cup, semi-final, 1970/71
5. **Liverpool 2 Tottenham Hotspur 2** UEFA Cup, semi-final, 1972/73
6. **Liverpool 3 Hibernian 2** UEFA Cup, first round, 1975/76
7. **Liverpool 7 Crusaders 0** European Cup, first round, 1976/77
8. **Liverpool 5 Aberdeen 0** European Cup, second round, 1980/81
9. **Liverpool 5 Dundalk 1** European Cup, first round, 1982/83
10. **Liverpool 2 Celtic 2** UEFA Cup, first round, 1997/98
11. **Liverpool 1 Celtic 3** UEFA Cup, quarter-final, 2002/03

BEST BOOKS

11 essential volumes for the well-read Red

1. Out Of His Skin, Dave Hill
This 1989 study of John Barnes, his impact on Liverpool and the pervasiveness of racism in the game and in society remains a compelling and thoughtful read.

2. Extra Time, Kevin Sampson
Nine months in the life of a Liverpool fan and Kevin Sampson, tracing the highs and lows of a frustrating 1997/98 season, featuring an eccentric supporting cast.

3. Ray Of Hope, Ray Kennedy and Dr Andrew Lees
The moving story of Liverpool's guileful 1970s midfielder, engagingly relating his battle against Parkinson's disease.

4. Faith Of Our Fathers, Alan Edge
The evocative tale of one devout fan's life growing up as a Red, through the glory years, the first seeds of hooliganism, Hillsborough and beyond. Funny and honest.

5. Billy Liddell, The Legend Who Carried The Kop, John Keith
The definitive biography of the greatest man to pull on the Red shirt, packed full of evocative memories from Liddell's team-mates, fans and family.

6. Hillsborough: The Truth, Phil Scaton
Detailed, harrowing account of the afternoon of 15 April 1989 and beyond, detailing the injustices and indignities of an aftermath that continues to this day.

7. Cup Kings 1965, Mark Platt
Unashamedly nostalgic round-by-round celebration of Liverpool's first FA Cup win, beautifully assembled and featuring fresh insight into the team of 1965.

8. Kennedy's Way, Alan Kennedy and John Williams
Excellent, revealing portrayal of life in the Liverpool dressing room, largely avoiding the clichés associated with the football biography.

9. Liverpool In Europe, Steve Hale and Ivan Ponting
Magnificent, comprehensive chronicle of Liverpool's travels from Reykjavik in 1964 to Dortmund in 2001, featuring photos, match reports, statistics and interviews.

10. The Boys From The Mersey, Nicky Allt
The readable, entertaining story of a Kirkby lad and his mates from the Anfield Road End as they travelled Europe, supporting the Reds and trailing havoc in their wake.

11. This Is Anfield, Andrew Thompson and Steve Hale
It costs £195 and is limited to 2,000 copies of a leather-bound deluxe edition, but this lavish, almost biblical club history, featuring Hale's iconic photos, is worth every penny.

BIGGEST WINS

11 occasions the teleprinter had to spell out Liverpool's result

1. Liverpool 11 Stromsgodset 0 Cup Winners' Cup, 1974
2. Liverpool 10 Dundalk 0 Inter-Cities Fairs Cup, 1969
3. Liverpool 10 Fulham 0 League Cup, 1986

4. Liverpool 10 Rotherham United 1 Division Two, 1896
5. Liverpool 10 Oulu Palloseura 1 European Cup, 1980
6. Liverpool 9 Newtown 0 FA Cup, 1892
7. Liverpool 9 Crystal Palace 0 Division One, 1989
8. Liverpool 8 Burnley 0 Division One, 1928
9. Liverpool 8 TSV Munich 0 Inter-Cities Fairs Cup, 1967
10. Liverpool 8 Swansea City 0 FA Cup, 1990
11. Liverpool 8 Stoke City 0 League Cup, 2000 (record away win)

BOB: IN HIS OWN WORDS

11 classic quotes from Bob Paisley

1. "If you're in the penalty area and don't know what to do with the ball, put it in the net and we'll discuss the options later."

2. "Mind, I've been here during the bad times too. One year we came second."

3. "I love the city and the people here. I've been with them for years and I fought alongside them. Ninety per cent of my regiment were from Merseyside. So I got to know the Liverpool character. From a psychological point of view, that was a big asset. I've had a fair time to judge the Liverpool people, and I think they're tremendous."

4. "I find out more about a player when he's injured. However much you try to involve him, he seems an outcast. You see the reaction, the character when a player is down."

5. "The whole of my life, what the supporters wanted was honesty. They were not so concerned with cultured football, but with triers who gave one hundred per cent."

6. "It's not about the long ball or the short ball. It's about the right ball."

7. "A lot of teams beat us, do a lap of honour and don't stop running. They live too long on one good result. I remember Jimmy Adamson crowing after Burnley beat us, that his players were in a different league. At the end of the season they were."

8. "Playing at Anfield lifts good professionals and puts the bad ones under pressure."

9. "Bill Shankly put steel tips on his shoes so people knew he was coming, whereas I'd be happy in my slippers."

10. "I let the players on the pitch do my talking for me."

11. "There's so many clubs been ruined by people's ego. The day after we won the European Cup, we were back at this club at 9.45 in the morning, talking about how we would do it again, working from that moment because nobody has the right to win anything they haven't earned."

BOGEY SIDES

That voodoo that they do so well. Curse them...

1. Crystal Palace
Forget the 9-0 the Eagles dumped us out of the FA Cup unforgettably in the 1990 semi-finals and again in the fourth round in 2003, as well as the League Cup in 1992.

2. Brighton and Hove Albion
The Seagulls sent us crashing out of the FA Cup on Sunday afternoons in 1983 and 1984, and claimed a draw at Anfield in 1991.

3. Wimbledon
Not just for that painful FA Cup final upset at the hands of the Crazy Gang in 1988, but also a total of seven league defeats in 14 seasons.

> FORGET THE 9-0 THE EAGLES DUMPED US OUT OF THE FA CUP IN 1990 AND IN THE FOURTH ROUND IN 2003

4. Nottingham Forest
For too long in the late 1970s, Cloughie's men had the upper hand on us, including that European Cup defeat and the 1978 League Cup final featuring Phil Thompson's 'professional foul' on John O'Hare.

5. Chelsea
Elvis Costello had it right when he sang *I Don't Want To Go To Chelsea*, thanks to a run of 13 trips to the Bridge without a single win between 1990 and 2003, plus FA Cup defeats in 1978, 1982 and 1997.

6. Leicester City
It was the Foxes who ended Liverpool's epic run of 85 matches unbeaten at home in 1981, and more recently beat us at Anfield three seasons running.

7. Everton
Included here due to a dismal run of 11 journeys across Stanley Park without a win between 1990 and 2000, including an FA Cup exit in 1991.

8. Leeds United
In the days when Revie and Shankly battled for supremacy of English football, they had the temerity to seal the championship at Anfield in 1969 and knocked us out of the Inter-Cities Fairs Cup in 1971.

9. Manchester United
Eric beating the Reds in white Armani in 1996, Strachan smoking a cigar in front of the Kop, Macari's deflection denying us the Treble in 1977, Yorke and Solskjaer stealing it in 1999…

10. Arsenal
From Charlie George celebrating on his back in 1971 to Charlie Nicholas ending Rushie's record in 1987 and Michael Thomas grabbing the title in the dying seconds in 1989, the Gunners like to upstage the Reds on the big occasion.

11. Luton Town
The Reds always hated playing on the Kenilworth Road carpet, winning on it just once between 1986 and 1992, including the annus horribilis of 1986/87, when we lost 4-1 in the league and 3-0 in the FA Cup.

BOOT-ROOM BOYS
The men behind the managers

1. Bob Paisley
A tireless wing-half for the Reds during the 1940s and 1950s, Paisley's tactical nous made him a natural to move into coaching when he hung up his boots. Initially putting his deep knowledge of physiotherapy into use as the club's spongeman, he graduated to first-team coach on Bill Shankly's arrival in 1959. Succeeding Shankly in 1974, Paisley would devote half a century of his life to Liverpool FC as player, coach, manager, director and adviser to Kenny Dalglish.

2. Joe Fagan
Uncle Joe arrived at Anfield as a trainer in 1958 after a playing career that peaked at Manchester City. It was Fagan who established a tiny 8ft x 8ft storeroom as

a de facto war room, albeit one furnished with boot racks and beer crates, and Fagan who laid down a training regime in detailed handwritten ledgers that became a footballing bible to be consulted for seasons to come. In 1974 he became Paisley's lieutenant, and assumed the mantle of manager himself nine seasons later while still living in his modest semi-detached house a few hundred yards from the club's Melwood training ground. Even Sven-Goran Eriksson learned at the shoulder of Fagan during an attachment at the club in the 1980s. He died in 2001.

3. Ronnie Moran

Nicknamed Bugsy, Moran went from schoolboy footballer for Liverpool to leading the team out at Wembley. Essentially the sergeant-major figure of the boot room, the uncompromising Moran joined the coaching staff in 1966 after a distinguished playing career in the red shirt. Initially a youth-team trainer, he became reserve team coach two years later, moving up to first-team coach in 1974. It was Moran who barked out the orders from the dugout, and Moran who would dish out the league championship medals with a reminder that pre-season training started on 16 July.

4. Tom Saunders

The former schoolteacher – best known as Liverpool's European reconnaissance man, travelling the continent to spy on forthcoming opponents and facilities – was initially appointed by Bill Shankly in 1968 as the first youth development officer at any league club. In 1993 he became a director of the club and vice-president, still offering counsel to Gerard Houllier during the Treble season. He died in 2001.

5. Roy Evans

Evans was just 25 and a fringe member of the Liverpool squad when, in 1974, he was offered the chance to become reserve team trainer. Even then, chairman John Smith predicted that Evans would one day manage the club. In nine seasons in charge of the reserves, he steered them to seven Central League championships, grooming many players for the first team. In 1983, he stepped up to join the first-team staff, first as trainer, then as assistant to Graeme Souness, before fulfilling Smith's prophecy in 1994.

6. Reuben Bennett

Previously manager at Motherwell, Ayr United and Third Lanark, the unsung Scot joined the Liverpool staff as first-team trainer during the club's lowest ebb in 1958, supervising training sessions throughout most of the Shankly era. In 1971 he was assigned a scouting role which he continued until 1983. He died in December 1989.

7. John Bennison

Bennison arrived at Anfield in 1970, initially as assistant to Tom Saunders, and stayed for 23 years. At first he looked after the schoolboy teams, grooming the likes of youth-team captain Phil Thompson for bigger and better things. He continued to work with the youngsters until 1983, when he took over Saunders's European duties, later assisting with the reserve team. He retired from football in 1993.

8. Geoff Twentyman

It's Twentyman who Liverpool fans should thank for spotting the potential of Ian Rush, Alan Hansen and Phil Neal, among many others. A centre-half for the Reds in the 1950s, he rejoined the club as chief scout in 1967 at the behest of Shankly, for whom he had played at Carlisle United. Blessed with one of the finest eyes for a footballer in England, he served the club until 1986.

9. Doug Livermore

Livermore made just a handful of appearances in midfield for Liverpool before joining Norwich, Bournemouth, Cardiff and Chester. He moved into coaching with Swansea under John Toshack, then Wales and Tottenham. In 1994 he returned to Anfield as assistant manager to Roy Evans. He left the club after five years when Gerard Houllier took over, and is now on the coaching staff at Norwich.

10. Sammy Lee

The tireless midfielder rejoined the club in 1993 to manage the reserve team, before being promoted to first-team coach by Gerard Houllier in 1999. Respected for his coaching skills, and for running a distinctive pre-match warm-up routine, he left the club in 2004 to take up a similar post at the FA with the England team, which he'd been helping part-time for several seasons.

11. Phil Thompson

Thommo had two spells on the coaching staff at the club he graced as one of its most decorated players. In 1986 he was appointed as reserve-team coach by Kenny Dalglish, but new manager Graeme Souness replaced him in 1992 with Sammy Lee. But in 1998 he returned as assistant to Gerard Houllier, regarded by some as a latter-day Ronnie Moran, and capably deputising for the Frenchman during his serious illness. However, the departure of Houllier in 2004 also saw Thompson leave, severing the final link to the old boot-room days.

BOY WONDER

11 great moments from Michael Owen's seven glorious seasons

1. The run and angled shot into Arsenal's bottom corner in the 2001 FA Cup final
2. The cool debut right-footed finish against Wimbledon in May 1997
3. The surge, shrug, loft and rubbed hands at St James' Park in 1998
4. The waltz through the Coventry City defence at Highfield Road in 2000
5. The curler into the corner at home to Boavista in 2001
6. The gallop and chip over the onrushing goalkeeper against Celtic in 1997
7. The deflected lob inside 21 seconds of coming on as sub at Liberec in 2000
8. The incredible double against Roma in the Stadio Olimpico in 2001
9. The 30-yard run and calm finish past Barthez in the 2003 League Cup final
10. The gravity-defying leap and header to make it 3-1 against Man United in 2001
11. That goal against Argentina at France 98 – England's finest World Cup strike

BRIEF ENCOUNTERS

Some will always be remembered… and some are best forgotten

1. Frank McGarvey 1979/80
Billed as Scotland's next big thing when he joined Liverpool from St Mirren in 1979, the striker only got as far as being named substitute and never actually got off the bench on any of those four occasions. Remarkably, he did appear for his country during his spell at Anfield, which ended when he signed for Celtic in 1980.

2. Wayne Harrison 1985-91
Bought from Oldham for £250,000, Harrison was the most expensive teenager at the time. Great things were expected from the prodigiously talented forward, but a series of crippling injuries meant that he never got to appear for the first team.

3. Mark Seagraves 1985-88
The defender enjoyed a high-profile debut for the Reds, appearing in a Milk Cup semi-final at QPR, screened live by the BBC. But he only made one more appearance for the club, in an FA Cup tie at York City.

4. Alex Watson 1986-91
The centre-half, younger brother of Everton defender Dave Watson, racked up just nine appearances in the red shirt, although one of them did come at Wembley in the 1988 Charity Shield against Wimbledon.

5. Alan Irvine 1986/87

Nicknamed Fraggle, the Scottish striker struggled to dislodge the established forwards after joining from Falkirk for £75,000. He made four appearances as a sub during his brief spell at the club, but he did enjoy one moment in the sun, tormenting the Everton defence during the 1987 League Cup tie at Goodison.

6. David Speedie 1990/91

Dalglish's final signing in 1991, the tempestuous Scottish striker had an amazing impact, netting an equaliser against Manchester United on his debut and scoring twice in the Anfield derby the next Saturday where he mistakenly celebrated in front of the Everton fans. In total, he played just 14 matches for the Reds.

7. Phil Charnock 1992-96

In 1992, aged 17 years and seven months, the midfielder became Liverpool's youngest-ever player to participate in European competition. He replaced Steve Harkness in a match against Apollon Limassol, but only started one more match.

8. Sean Dundee 1998/99

Born in South Africa, the striker earned one cap as a naturalised German after some impressive form in the Bundesliga, but he looked completely out of his depth in his five substitute appearances for Liverpool.

9. Jean-Michel Ferri 1998/99

The French midfielder was signed from Turkish club Istanbulspor for £1.5m as cover for Paul Ince in 1999, but struggled to impress. He made only two substitute performances in the Premiership before being hastily shipped out to Sochaux.

10. Bernard Diomede 2000-03

Dio-Dio was a member of France's 1998 World Cup squad, but the wingman never made the breakthrough at Anfield after a £3m transfer from Auxerre. He made just five appearances, only one of them as a starter in the Premiership (against Sunderland). He left on a free to join Ajaccio.

11. Nicolas Anelka 2001/02

The temperamental French striker arrived in 2001 from Paris St Germain on a loan deal, but five goals in 22 appearances just wasn't enough of a return to persuade the Reds to sign him, despite an electrifying performance on a memorable night against Newcastle United at Anfield.

CHAMPIONSHIPS

"It was our bread and butter", said Shanks. Here's 11 that live in the memory

1. 1900/01
The Reds just needed a point from their last match to overhaul rivals Sunderland but clinched their first league championship with a tense 1-0 victory at West Bromwich Albion, courtesy of a John Walker strike. The team was welcomed back to Merseyside in a horse-drawn carriage by a fife and drum band playing *The Conquering Hero*.

2. 1922/23
Liverpool's third championship, and their second in two years, was based on a solid defence that conceded a record low of 31 goals in 42 matches, and a haul of 70 goals, 22 of them from the boots of Harry Chambers. The Reds finished six points ahead of their nearest rivals, Sunderland.

3. 1946/47
George Kay's team didn't secure the championship until June, the first post-war season being extended after some appalling winter weather. Manchester United, Wolves and Stoke had all looked better placed, but despite only playing at home twice in their last seven fixtures, the Reds clinched it by a point, beating Wolves on the final day as Stoke lost to Sheffield United.

4. 1963/64
After Bill Shankly's team had made an erratic start with just one victory in their first four games, the Reds effectively clinched the title from Manchester United with three wins over Easter. Roger Hunt and Ian St John spearheaded a majestic team that scored 92 goals in 42 matches.

5. 1972/73
Liverpool had been cruelly denied the championship on the last day of the previous season, but made no mistake in 1972/73, failing to score in just four matches and

losing just once at Anfield. The 2-0 defeat of Leeds in April confirms the title, and the trophy is handed over before the last match at home to Leicester.

6. 1975/76
Following a season-long battle with a talented QPR side featuring Gerry Francis and Stan Bowles, the Reds needed to win their final match at relegation-threatened Wolves to overhaul the Londoners, who watched from a London TV studio. At a packed Molineux the Reds trailed at half-time, but Keegan, Toshack and Kennedy secured the championship, and the party lasts all the way back up the M6.

7. 1978/79
Perhaps the most dominant team in championship history, Paisley's mighty Reds went top on the second Saturday of the season and stayed there. They lost just four matches, none at home; conceded 16 goals, just four of them at Anfield; and used just 15 players. The stand-out match was the merciless 7-0 thrashing of a promoted Tottenham that contained Ardiles, Villa and all.

8. 1981/82
Liverpool's most satisfying title to date. The Reds languished in 13th place after a 3-1 defeat to Manchester City on Boxing Day, but five consecutive wins signalled a New Year turnaround, as the Reds steadily climbed the table. Eleven straight wins in the spring and the emergence of Ian Rush secured the championship trophy, the old lady herself being flung around at Anfield by Souness and Whelan.

9. 1983/84
In 1984 the Reds became the third club to win three league championships in a row, finishing top with 80 points at the end of a nine-month procession. The title is secured with a goalless draw at Notts County, Joe Fagan's side eventually finishing three points ahead of nearest challengers Southampton.

> **PAISLEY'S MIGHTY REDS WENT TOP ON THE SECOND SATURDAY OF THE SEASON AND STAYED THERE**

10. 1985/86
Manchester United had raced out of the blocks with ten straight wins before Everton assumed control of the title race. It was, reckoned Alan Hansen in mid-season, the worst Liverpool side he'd ever played in, but a fantastic revival saw the Reds enter the battle. The balance of power shifted one dramatic night when the Blues lost to Oxford and Liverpool beat Leicester, before Kenny settled it on the final Saturday at Stamford Bridge. Manchester United finished fourth…

11. 1987/88

Liverpool went 29 matches unbeaten from the start of the 1987/88 season, equalling Leeds United's record. They couldn't beat it, however, thanks to Everton's Wayne Clarke. It was one of only two defeats that season, as the Reds wrapped it up with a 1-0 win against Spurs, finishing with 90 points from 40 matches.

CHARITY SHIELD VICTORIES

11 traditional curtain-raisers

1. **Liverpool 2 West Ham 2** shared, 1964
2. **Liverpool 1 Everton 0** 1966
3. **Liverpool 1 Leeds United 1** won 6-5 on penalties, 1974
4. **Liverpool 1 Southampton 0** 1976
5. **Liverpool 3 Arsenal 1** 1979
6. **Liverpool 1 West Ham United 0** 1980
7. **Liverpool 1 Tottenham Hotspur 0** 1982
8. **Liverpool 1 Everton 1** shared, 1986
9. **Liverpool 2 Wimbledon 1** 1988
10. **Liverpool 1 Arsenal 0** 1989
11. **Liverpool 2 Manchester United 1** 2001

CHRISTMAS CHEERS

"Oh, come let us adore them." 11 wins over the festive period

1. Liverpool 2 Charlton Athletic 0 28 December 1959
The Reds gain their first victory under new manager Bill Shankly, as Alan A'Court and Roger Hunt get on the score sheet in this Division Two encounter.

2. Liverpool 2 Chelsea 1 24 and 26 December 1966
Christmas comes early at Stamford Bridge as Marvin Hinton puts through his own net. Geoff Strong nets the other as the Reds defeat the Blues 2-1. Then, on Boxing Day, they do it again at Anfield thanks to Willie Stevenson and Roger Hunt.

3. Burnley 1 Liverpool 5 26 December 1969
Liverpool thrash the Clarets in front of 22,944 at Turf Moor, with Ian Ross, Bobby Graham, Chris Lawler, Peter Thompson and Ian Callaghan on the score sheet.

4. Liverpool 4 Manchester City 1 26 December 1974
Brian Hall nets twice in this Boxing Day romp, with Steve Heighway and John Toshack completing the scoring to avenge their defeat at Maine Road in September.

5. Liverpool 4 Stoke City 0 27 December 1976
The Reds consolidate their position at the top of the table. Phil Thompson opens the scoring after just five minutes before Phil Neal, Kevin Keegan and David Johnson secure the two points.

6. Manchester United 0 Liverpool 3 26 December 1978
The Reds mount an exhibition of total football, netting their biggest post-war win at Old Trafford courtesy of goals from Ray Kennedy, Jimmy Case and David Fairclough.

7. Liverpool 2 Manchester United 0 26 December 1979
"There's only one United – and that's a chocolate biscuit!" Alan Hansen had the Boxing Day crowd singing when he put the Reds in front after 15 minutes, and David Johnson wrapped up the victory five minutes from the end.

8. Liverpool 5 Manchester City 2 27 December 1982
Twelve months earlier, City had left Liverpool languishing in 13th place, but Kenny Dalglish avenged that defeat with a hat-trick. Phil Neal and Ian Rush completed the scoring.

9. Oxford United 0 Liverpool 3 26 December 1987
Kenny Dalglish's men clock up their 20th consecutive unbeaten match of the glorious 1987/88 season. Goals from John Aldridge, John Barnes and Steve McMahon confirm their superiority at the Manor Ground.

10. Liverpool 4 Newcastle United 2 28 December 1998
The Reds were two goals down with just 23 minutes remaining, but two each from Michael Owen and Karl-Heinz Riedle ensured a thrilling fight back as Dietmar Hamann is sent off for Newcastle.

11. West Bromwich Albion 0 Liverpool 5 26 December 2004
Two goals from John-Arne Riise crowned Liverpool's rout of the Baggies on Boxing Night. Florent Sinama-Pongolle, Steven Gerrard and Luis Garcia scored the rest. Milan Baros even missed a penalty.

CLASSIC KITS: HOME

11 sartorial triumphs – and disasters – as worn by Anfield's finest

1. Blue and white 1892
Remarkable as it now might seem, the first Liverpool kit featured blue and white quarters and white shorts. This wasn't, as you might guess, a hangover from the split with Everton, as the Toffees then played in ruby shirts.

2. Red and white late 1890s
The exact date is unknown, but some time towards the end of the 19th century, the club decided to change its strip to red shirts with white shorts, a combination that was to last for six decades.

3. Badge and v-neck collar 1950s
Liverpool's strip evolved through the years and it wasn't until the 1950s, when the club found itself in Division Two, that the Liver Bird appeared permanently on the red shirt. It was around this time that the collar was exchanged for a v-neck design.

> THE ADVERT DEPICTED KENNY AND CO PLAYING HEAD TENNIS OVER THE BONNET OF A TALBOT SUNBEAM

4. Shankly's all-red 1954
In December 1964, Liverpool changed to red shorts for a European Cup tie at Anderlecht at the behest of Bill Shankly. He believed it had the psychological effect of making the players look bigger, recruiting a reluctant Ron Yeats into modelling the new kit for the team. A classic was born.

5. Umbro/Hitachi 1979
Liverpool became the first professional team in England to display shirt sponsorship in 1979, signing a deal with the Japanese electronics firm. The Umbro diamond logo had first appeared on the shirt in 1975.

6. Umbro/pinstripes 1982
The first fundamental change in 90 years came in 1982, with the addition of white pinstripes. Crown Paints had taken over the sponsorship, and their logo appeared on the shirts, with a smaller version to meet television sponsorship restrictions.

7. Adidas/the Double kit 1985
In the mid-1980s, Adidas took over the kit contract. Their first design, featuring a Liver Bird 'contra shadow', made its debut in the 1985 European Cup final. It was the

kit worn as the Reds won the Double, although there were variations, some shirts bearing the Crown Paints logo on just one line, not two.

8. Adidas/white streaks 1989
As football kits became more and more outlandish in the late 1980s, a revolutionary new Liverpool kit – featuring white paint streaks all over the shirt, plus the logo of latest sponsors Candy – appeared in time for the club's 18th championship.

9. Adidas/three stripes 1991
The summer of 1991 heralded a radical new design, featuring three broad Adidas stripes across the right shoulder and on the shorts. In 1992, the logo of new sponsors Carlsberg appeared on the shirts, as well as a new badge, to coincide with the club's centenary season.

10. Adidas/v-neck 1995
Adidas's best kit for Liverpool was also their last, returning to basics in 1995 with a refined, uncluttered design, moving the Adidas stripes back to the sleeves and a v-neck that resembled a cricket jumper. It only lasted one season, but is fondly remembered to this day.

11. Reebok/collar 1996
Reebok took over as kit manufacturer in 1996, bringing back a collar for the first time in 40 years, and setting the badge in an oval, another throwback to the 1950s. It was memorably amended for a tour of Norway, where alcohol advertising is forbidden, replacing Carlsberg with "Probably…"

COMMERCIAL BREAKS

From aftershave to isotonic drinks, the stars who turned salesman

1. Kevin Keegan
K.K. teamed up with Henry Cooper in 1975 to promote the "great smell" of Brut 33, exhorting us to "splash it all over". Around the same time, he appeared in a public information film made outside Anfield to promote the Green Cross Code.

2. Kenny Dalglish
In 1978 Scotland's World Cup squad promoted Talbot cars in a memorable advert depicting Kenny and co playing head tennis over the bonnet of a Sunbeam.

3. Ian Rush

Everyone remembers the "Ian Rush told me, if I didn't drink milk, I'd only be good enough to play for Accrington Stanley" commercial. But he wasn't actually in it. He did, however, appear in a 1985 ad for Nike, in which he was seen being 'created' as a superhuman in a Professor Frankenstein-like laboratory.

4. John Barnes

Digger fronted a campaign for Lucozade Sport in 1990, describing the drink as just the thing after "90 minutes of sheer hell" and introducing a generation of impressionable kids to the word "isotonic".

5. Bruce Grobbelaar and Paul Stewart

The duo appeared in the "Whole New Ball" game campaign for Sky Sports in 1992, Brucie juggling and spinning a ball on his finger and Stewart driving a red Porsche to the strains of *Alive And Kicking* by Simple Minds.

6. Ian St John

The Saint teamed up with his TV sidekick Jimmy Greaves for a remake of the classic R. Whites Secret Lemonade Drinker commercial. The memorable song was written by the father of Liverpool fan Elvis Costello.

7. Jason McAteer

Trigger starred in an advert for Head & Shoulders shampoo, accompanied by an impressive voiceover declaring "Jason knows he can have it all!"

8. Robbie Fowler

God teamed up with the likes of Ian Wright and Eric Cantona for a classic Nike ad in 1996, featuring Premiership stars playing alongside Sunday leaguers on Hackney Marshes, to the soundtrack of Blur's *Park Life*.

9. Michael Owen

Predictably, Owen has been sought out for a string of commercials. These included one for British Airways alongside the likes of John Lennon and Damon Hill; one for Persil ("Thanks, mum!") and another for Walkers Crisps.

10. Alan Hansen

Jocky has appeared in a few commercials, including one for Littlewoods Pools and, more recently, starred as a butler cleaning football boots and serving up pints in a campaign for Carlsberg.

11. Steven Gerrard
In 2005, Stevie G followed in the footsteps of Barnes and Owen by starring in a campaign for Lucozade Sport, highlighting its benefits to "the Midfield Engine" in a technologically impressive commercial.

CONTINENTAL REDS
They took their skills to Europe. For some, it was like playing in a foreign country

1. **Phil Babb** Sporting Lisbon
2. **David Fairclough** Lucerne, Beveren
3. **Kevin Keegan** Hamburg
4. **Sammy Lee** Osasuna
5. **Steve McManaman** Real Madrid
6. **Michael Owen** Real Madrid
7. **Michael Robinson** Osasuna
8. **Ian Rush** Juventus
9. **Dean Saunders** Benfica, Galatasaray
10. **Michael Thomas** Benfica
11. **Barry Venison** Galatasaray

CULT HEROES
11 men who won the hearts of the Kopites

1. Albert Stubbins
"ALB! ERT! Albert Stubbins is the man for me!" The legendary striker hit 83 goals for the Reds in the 1940s and 1950s, appeared on the cover of *Sergeant Pepper* in the 1960s and inspired his own cult movement at Anfield in the 1990s, the Albert Stubbins Crazy Crew.

2. Gerry Byrne
Perhaps the bravest man to wear the Liver Bird, Byrne played for 117 minutes of the 1965 FA Cup final against Leeds United with a broken collarbone sustained during an early challenge. That in an era when there were no substitutes.

3. Joey Jones
The spirit of the Kop embodied in a fist-clenching, tattooed defensive warrior, and

immortalised in the legendary banner "Joey Ate The Frogs Legs, Made The Swiss Roll, Now He's Munching Gladbach" at the 1977 European Cup final.

4. Avi Cohen
Never truly fulfilled his promise at Anfield, but his performance in the 1980 title decider against Aston Villa earned him cult status. The defender netted an own goal in front of the Kop, before bursting out of nowhere to put the Reds back in front.

5. Bruce Grobbelaar
Not just for the spaghetti legs in Rome, but also for the handstands at Wembley, the star jumps as the PA announced "Operation Exercise Anfield", for wearing a cap with a rubber duck on it, for balancing an umbrella on his nose, and much, much more.

6. Howard Gayle
Just five games for Liverpool but his performance as a sub against Bayern Munich in 1981 conferred cult status on the club's first black player. He put so much energy into running the German defence ragged he had to be substituted himself.

7. Jan Molby
Rambo became a hero at Anfield, not just for his vision and defence-splitting balls, but for his Danish/Scouse accent and a fund of classic anecdotes, including one about him getting a lift home aboard a fire engine after a night out…

8. Ronnie Rosenthal
He might have been tagged "super-sub", but the Israeli striker deserved much more, thanks to some improbable deeds, including a hat-trick on his full debut and a last-minute winner against Everton at the Kop end in 1993 that had the entire team bath singing his name.

9. Titi Camara
Full of skill and little tricks, Titi never quite managed to fit in at Liverpool. But his performance against West Ham in 1999 on the day his father died, tearfully scoring an emotional winner, makes him a Red hero.

10. Erik Meijer
He scored just two goals for Liverpool, and they were against Hull City. But just the mention of Mad Erik can make any Red smile, not least for turning up at the 2001 UEFA Cup final to support his old club, having a pint with the fans in the Altermarkt and leading them to the Westfalenstadion like the pied piper.

11. Igor Biscan
"Eeeeeeeegor!" Anfield has taken the Croatian midfield dynamo to its heart, thanks to some bustling performances in Europe and some unlikely goals, including a memorable blast at Fulham in 2004.

CUP UPSETS

From third-round banana skins to semi-final shockers, 11 afternoons to forget

1. **Gateshead 1 Liverpool 0** FA Cup 1953
2. **Worcester City 2 Liverpool 1** FA Cup 1959
3. **Liverpool 1 Swansea City 2** FA Cup 1964
4. **Watford 1 Liverpool 0** FA Cup 1970
5. **Liverpool 1 Brighton & Hove Albion 2** FA Cup 1983
6. **Liverpool 3 Crystal Palace 4** FA Cup 1990
7. **Peterborough 1 Liverpool 0** League Cup 1992
8. **Liverpool 0 Bolton Wanderers 2** FA Cup 1993
9. **Liverpool 0 Bristol City 1** FA Cup 1994
10. **Liverpool 1 Grimsby 2** League Cup 2002
11. **Burnley 1 Liverpool 0** FA Cup 2005

DEADLY DOUBLE ACTS

11 great Liverpool partnerships

1. **Ian Rush and Kenny Dalglish** 1981-90
2. **Roger Hunt and Ian St John** 1961-70
3. **Kevin Keegan and John Toshack** 1971-77
4. **Alan Hansen and Mark Lawrenson** 1981-88
5. **Jack Balmer and Albert Stubbins** 1946-52
6. **Sami Hyypia and Stephane Henchoz** 1999-2005
7. **Peter Beardsley and John Aldridge** 1987-1989

8. Ian Rush and Robbie Fowler 1993-96
9. Emlyn Hughes and Phil Thompson 1971-79
10. Michael Owen and Emile Heskey 2000-04
11. Larry Lloyd and Tommy Smith 1969-74

DEBUG SCORERS

Eleven Reds who netted in their first game

1. Billy Liddell v Chester City, 1946
2. Albert Stubbins v Bolton Wanderers, 1946
3. Jimmy Melia v Nottingham Forest, 1955
4. Roger Hunt v Scunthorpe United, 1959
5. Alun Evans v Leicester City, 1968
6. Kevin Keegan v Nottingham Forest, 1971
7. Ray Kennedy v Chelsea, 1974
8. Sammy Lee v Leicester City, 1978
9. Ronnie Whelan v Stoke City, 1981
10. Stan Collymore v Sheffield Wednesday, 1995
11. Abel Xavier v Ipswich Town, 2002

DREAM DERBIES

11 memories to treasure of the days we played the Toffees for a laugh

1. Liverpool 2 Everton 2 17 November 1894
Thirty thousand flat-capped Scousers headed down Walton Breck Road to witness
the first Anfield derby since Everton handed back the keys to the ground in a row
over the rent and moved across the park to Goodison. The Toffees had beaten
Liverpool 3-0 at home in the first match a month earlier, and took a first-half lead
at Anfield. Liverpool pulled one back early in the second half through David
Hannah, but were losing 2-1 when they were awarded a penalty in the 90th minute.
Scotsman Jimmy Ross stepped up to rescue a point for the Reds. It was the start
of a beautiful relationship.

2. Everton 0 Liverpool 4 FA Cup fourth round, 29 January 1955
Liverpool had been relegated from Division One at the end of the previous season,
rendering this FA Cup tie the only derby of the season. And, in front of 72,000 fans at

DOUBLE WINNERS 1986

Grobbelaar

Nicol Hansen Lawrenson Beglin

Johnston Molby MacDonald Whelan

Dalglish

Rush

The team that beat Everton 3-1 in the 1986 FA Cup final on 10 May 1986 – having also beaten their near neighbours to the championship the week before.

Goodison Park, the Reds rubbed their neighbours' noses in a humiliating defeat that remains the greatest upset in derby history to this day. First-half goals from Billy Liddell and Alan A'Court put Liverpool in front, before John Evans grabbed two after the break. "Everton were defeated by their tragic over-eagerness to win this white-hot derby tie," read the improbable match report in the *Sunday Express*.

3. Liverpool 3 Everton 2 21 November 1970
Everton were leading 2-0 with just 27 minutes left when Steve Heighway cut mesmerisingly through their defence to pull one back. He also created the second, delivering a cross which John Toshack headed home to net his first for Liverpool and level the scores. Attacking towards a deafening Kop, the Reds weren't settling for the draw, and with just six minutes left, Tosh flicked on an Alec Lindsay free kick enabling Chris Lawler to fire in the winner off the post. Pure ecstasy and an epic comeback.

4. Liverpool 2 Everton 1 FA Cup semi-final, 27 March 1971
In March 1971 Merseyside travelled to Old Trafford for this FA Cup semi-final and it was Everton who got off to a flier, Alan Ball putting the Blues in front on 15 minutes. Liverpool had played in a delayed Fairs Cup tie at Bayern Munich just 48 hours earlier and got their game together once Shankly had told them to get the ball on

the deck. It had been in the air so much, he said, the midfield would need a ladder. Alun Evans put them level before Brian Hall pounced on Andy Rankin's fumble to send the Reds to Wembley.

5. Liverpool 2 Everton 2 FA Cup semi-final, 23 April 1977
They still haven't forgiven Clive Thomas at Goodison. Liverpool were fighting for silverware on three fronts when the FA's velvet bag paired them with the Blues at Maine Road. Terry McDermott gave Bob Paisley's men the lead in the rain with a beautiful lob over David Lawson, before Duncan McKenzie equalised. Jimmy Case restored Liverpool's lead, only for Bruce Rioch to equalise. Then, in a moment that leaves Everton fans incandescent with rage to this day, Bryan Hamilton looked to have snatched it for the Blues at the death, only for idiosyncratic Welsh whistle-blower Thomas to disallow it for some never-adequately-explained reason. The Reds made no mistake in the replay, winning 3-0.

6. Liverpool 2 Everton 2 20 October 1979
Best remembered for a mass brawl in the first half, as Souness, Case and Kennedy squared up to Lyons, Higgins and Latchford, but the highlight was some fearsome handbagging from drinking buddies Terry McDermott and Gary Stanley that earned both an early bath, Stanley somehow managing to damage one of Terry Mac's precious sovereigns with a tooth. Ray Kennedy and a Mike Lyons own goal earned a point for Bob Paisley's men, and to round off a perfect afternoon, a female streaker.

7. Everton 0 Liverpool 5 6 November 1982
A date engraved on the heart of every true Red, and no doubt on that of Glenn Keeley, the Everton defender sent off for a professional foul on his one and only appearance for the Blues. But the star of the day was a rampant Ian Rush, netting a hatful against the team he supported as a Flint teenager. The supernatural relationship between predator Rush and creator supreme Kenny Dalglish was in full effect as Liverpool racked up the biggest away win in a derby for 72 years. It was a feat celebrated in song on the Kop ever since, for this was the match in which Liverpool played the Toffees for a laugh and left them feeling blue, as Rush scored one, Rush scored two, Rush scored three and Rush scored four, la la la…

8. Everton 4 Liverpool 4 FA Cup fifth-round replay, 20 February 1991
Kenny Dalglish's last match as Liverpool manager. Not a bad way to bow out, even if this replay probably contributed somewhat to the stress that prompted him to quit. Four times the Reds took the lead, only for a Tony Cottee-inspired Everton to keep pegging them back. The real highlight, the best of many, was John Barnes's strike from 20 yards at the Gwladys Street end which curled effortlessly over the

Blues defence, Neville Southall's head and into the corner of the net. If you're going to go, go out in style.

9. Liverpool 3 Everton 2 3 April 1999

Liverpool hadn't beaten the Blues in five long years, and with no silverware on the immediate horizon, these things mattered more than ever. It looked like Everton would retain alehouse bragging rights when Olivier Dacourt gave them the lead with a pile-driver after just 40 seconds. But Robbie Fowler nabbed two to put the Reds 2-1 in front. (The second, from the spot, is best remembered for Robbie's infamous line-sniffing celebration in front of the Everton fans in defiance of their drug-taking chants.) Patrik Berger looked like he'd sealed it after 82 minutes of an 18-rated derby but Franny Jeffers grabbed one back for Everton. The Reds were clinging on to their three points when Danny Cadamarteri sent a shot goalwards, but on the line was new Academy graduate Steven Gerrard to clear it to safety. Stevie celebrated arms aloft as if he'd just scored himself.

10. Everton 2 Liverpool 3 16 April 2001

In one of the most dramatic Easter revivals in 2,000 years, Liverpool kept their bid for Champions League football alive and Gary McAllister secured his place in Anfield immortality. Houllier's men had taken an early lead through Emile Heskey before Duncan Ferguson levelled just before half-time. Markus Babbel restored Liverpool's lead after the break. One minute later, the Reds had the chance to extend their lead but Fowler hit the post with a controversial penalty. It was all getting a bit frenzied when Igor Biscan was sent off, and just nine minutes remained when the Blues were awarded another dubious penalty. David Unsworth converted and it looked like the Champions League was slipping away, when, in the 94th minute, McAllister stepped up to blast a laser-guided free kick past Paul Gerrard. Cue absolute mayhem.

11. Liverpool 2 Everton 1 20 March 2005

The most intense derby in years, with Everton for once looking down on Liverpool as both sides scrabbled over fourth place. Liverpool, having stuttered all season, showed what they could do with some slick passing, and a free kick blast from Steven Gerrard put the Reds in front before Luis Garcia followed up from an improbable lob by Fernando Morientes that Nigel Martyn could only parry. Milan Baros might have extended Liverpool's lead but amid a frantic atmosphere and some extremely physical challenges from the one-time School of Science, it was ironic that Baros had to walk for an admittedly appalling foul on Alan Stubbs. Tim Cahill drilled one back for Everton, but the Reds hung on for a satisfying victory as Everton boss David Moyes frothed embarrassingly about getting "his people" to look into the lack of injury time.

EARLY DAYS

11 baggy-shorted heroes from before World War 1

1. Harry Bradshaw 1893-98
The courageous and adaptable frontman secured Liverpool promotion to Division One for the first time with a goal against Newton Heath in 1894. He only got one cap for Ireland but he was the first Liverpool player to gain international recognition.

2. Malcolm McVean 1893-97
The Scot holds the distinction of netting Liverpool's first league goal – against Middlesbrough Ironopolis in 1893. Blessed with blistering pace, the forward had been an apprentice shipyard boilermaker before becoming a footballer. McVean also scored a hat-trick in the club's record league win, 10-1 against Rotherham.

3. Joe McQue 1893-98
The rock at the heart of the club's first successful team, McQue joined the club from Celtic in 1893 and rarely missed a game in his five seasons at Anfield, grabbing his share of goals from defence. McQue was granted a testimonial match in 1896.

LIVERPOOL'S FIRST ENGLAND CAPTAIN. LONGWORTH WAS EASILY RECOGNISABLE THANKS TO HIS HAIR

4. Rab Howell 1898-1901
Born in a caravan in Sheffield, Howell is believed to be the only Romany to have represented England. The tireless right-half, who stood just 5ft 5in, joined the club from Sheffield United in 1898 for £200.

5. Alex Raisbeck 1898-1909
The commanding Scottish defender, once described as "pulsating to the fingertips with the joy of life", was signed from Stoke after the club chairman put manager Tom Watson on a train and told him not to return without him. Raisbeck was a regular in the first championship team of 1901, and worked as the club's billboard inspector.

6. Jack Parkinson 1899-1914
The lethal goalscorer from Bootle made his Liverpool debut against Everton in 1899 and spent 12 seasons at Anfield, his most successful campaign coming in 1909/10 when he topped the league scoring table with 30 goals.

7. Sam Raybould 1899-1907
Recruited from New Brighton Tower, Raybould once scored against Everton after just 30 seconds and in 1905 became the first Liverpool player to net a hat-trick against Manchester United. He scored 127 goals in 224 games for the club.

8. Arthur Goddard 1901-14
Branded "Graceful Arthur" by fans due to his stylish performances on the right-wing, he clocked up 415 appearances in 13 seasons, earning a deserved benefit match.

9. Donald McKinley 1909-29
The Scot filled practically every outfield role in almost 20 years at the club, but his best position was in defence, becoming an overlapping full-back decades before the term had been thought of. Deadly from set-pieces: it is said he once scored a free kick against West Ham from his own half.

10. Ephraim Longworth 1910-28
Liverpool's first England captain was instantly recognisable due to the lock of hair hanging over his forehead. Longworth was a defensive craftsman who preferred to build an attack rather than just clearing his lines. He served the club for 18 years until he was 40, and later joined the coaching staff.

11. Billy Lacey 1911-24
Blessed with a distinctive chin frequently caricatured by the football cartoonists, the tricky winger arrived at Anfield in a swap deal with Everton. The skilful Irishman won two championship medals for the club and appeared in the 1914 FA Cup final.

END-TO-ENDERS

11 classic matches that kept the fans entertained

1. Liverpool 4 Birmingham City 3 1965
2. Liverpool 4 Birmingham City 3 1972
3. Liverpool 5 Stoke City 3 1976
4. Liverpool 4 Nottingham Forest 3 1982

5. Leeds United 4 Liverpool 5 1991
6. Liverpool 4 Chesterfield 4 1991
7. Liverpool 4 Newcastle United 3 1996
8. Liverpool 6 FC Sion 3 1996
9. Liverpool 4 Newcastle United 3 1997
10. Liverpool 4 Blackburn Rovers 3 2002
11. Fulham 2 Liverpool 4 2004

EUROPEAN MISSIONS

"Attack! Attack! Attack attack attack!" 11 continental classics

1. Cologne European Cup second round, 24 March 1965
Three hours of football had failed to separate the two teams and in the days before penalty shoot-outs, deadlocked ties were settled by a play-off on neutral territory. But the replay ended 2-2, the tie to be settled by the toss of a disc. On the first toss, it got stuck in the mud, but on the second throw it came down red for Liverpool.

2. Celtic Cup Winners' Cup semi-final, 19 April 1966
The Reds had lost the first leg 1-0 at Celtic Park thanks to a Bobby Lennox goal. With thousands of Glaswegians descending on Anfield, the odds were stacked against Liverpool. But strikes from Tommy Smith and Geoff Strong saw off Jock Stein's men.

3. Bruges UEFA Cup final, 28 April 1976
Having beaten Barcelona in the semis, Liverpool might have thought they'd done the hard part, but in the first leg of the final at Anfield they were two down after just 12 minutes. In the second half, however, a Keegan-inspired revival saw the Reds make it 3-2 in the space of just five minutes.

4. St Etienne European Cup quarter-final, 16 March 1977
The French champions were one of Europe's finest teams, having reached the final the previous season, and won the first leg 1-0. The Reds were fired up for the return but Robert Bathenay's away goal looked as if it would be decisive until Bob Paisley flung on Davie Fairclough, whose 84th-minute winner sent Liverpool into raptures.

5. Bayern Munich European Cup semi-final, 22 April 1981
The Germans looked to have secured a distinct advantage, earning a goalless draw at Anfield in the first leg. And when Dalglish had to limp off early in the second match, things looked bleak. But his replacement, Howard Gayle, ran rings around

11. EUROPEAN CUP WINNERS 1977

Clemence

Neal   Smith   Hughes   Jones

Kennedy   Case   Callaghan   Heighway

Keegan   Toshack (Fairclough)

Liverpool are crowned champions of Europe for the first time beating St Etienne 3-1 on 16 March 1977.

Bayern and Liverpool made the breakthrough on 83 minutes through Ray Kennedy. Rummenigge pulled one back to make it 1-1 but the away goal made it irrelevant.

6. Roma European Cup final, 30 May 1984
Forced to play the final on the home ground of their opponents, Liverpool hit back with their secret weapon… Chris Rea. A rousing singalong of *I Don't Know What It Is But I Love It* in the tunnel unnerves the Italians. Extra time fails to separate the sides at 1-1 but despite Steve Nicol's agonising shootout miss, the Reds win 4-2 on penalties.

7. Auxerre UEFA Cup second round, 6 November 1991
There were only 23,094 at Anfield to witness it, but it sounded like twice as many as Liverpool recovered from a two-goal deficit in a European first leg for the first time in their history. Molby's early penalty set the revival rolling. Mike Marsh's equaliser put victory within reach, and Mark Walters's late winner made the Kop explode.

8. Roma Champions League, 19 March 2002
Back among Europe's elite for the first time since 1985, the Reds needed a two-goal win against Roma to progress. Gerard Houllier's return from heart surgery inspired Liverpool to an emphatic 2-0 win, Jari Litmanen and Emile Heskey netting the goals.

9. Basle Champions League, 12 November 2002
The Reds need an away win against the Swiss champions in their final group match to reach the last 16. Three-nil down after 29 minutes, they look dead and buried, but second-half goals from Murphy and Owen set up the fightback. Owen sees an 85th-minute penalty saved, rolls in the rebound, but Houllier's team can't find the winner.

10. Olympiakos Champions League, 8 December 2004
The equation for Rafael Benitez is clear: Liverpool must beat Olympiakos by two goals to reach the last 16. Rivaldo's first-half goal looks to have put paid to that idea, but a quick burst of *YNWA* before the second half is the prelude to an amazing comeback. Goals from Sinama-Pongolle, Mellor and an unerring 86th-minute thunderbolt from Gerrard in front of the Kop achieve the vital margin.

11. AC Milan, UEFA Champions League final, 25 May 2005
Three-nil down at the interval, the Reds face perhaps their toughest Mission Impossible ever. But in the space of six spine-tingling minutes at the start of the second half, Liverpool haul the score back to 3-3, before the agony of the penalty lottery. But Dietmar Hamann, Vladimir Smicer and Djibril Cisse dispatch their kicks past shoot-out specialist Dida, while Jerzy Dudek's spaghetti legged antics prompted Serginho to blast his shot over the bar, before saving from Pirlo and crucially, Shevchenko, to secure an incredible triumph.

EXALTED EUROPEAN RIVALS

11 fellow aristocrats we've met more than once

1. Celtic Cup Winners' Cup 1965/66; UEFA Cup 1997/98, 2002/03
2. Juventus Cup Winners' Cup 1965/66; Super Cup 1985; European Cup 1984/85, 2004/05
3. Borussia Dortmund Cup Winners' Cup 1965/66; Champions League 2001/02
4. Atletico Bilbao Inter-Cities Fairs Cup 1968/69; European Cup 1983/84
5. Borussia Moenchengladbach UEFA Cup 1972/73; European Cup 1976/77, 1977/78
6. Bayern Munich Inter-Cities Fairs Cup 1970/71; Cup Winners' Cup 1971/72; European Cup 1980/81; Super Cup 2001
7. FC Bruges UEFA Cup 1975/75; European Cup 1977/78
8. Barcelona UEFA Cup 1975/76, 2000/01; Champions League 2001/02
9. Benfica European Cup 1977/78, 1983/84, 1984/85
10. CSKA Sofia European Cup 1980/81, 1981/82
11. Roma European Cup 1983/84, 2001/02

FA CUP FINALS

11 memorable moments from Wembley, Cardiff and Crystal Palace

1. Liverpool 0 Burnley 1 24 April 1914
Played in front of King George V and 72,778 spectators at Crystal Palace, Liverpool's first FA Cup final ends in failure. The Reds dominate but fail to make the most of their chances, only for Bertie Freeman to score for the Clarets on a breakaway.

2. Liverpool 0 Arsenal 2 29 April 1950
The Reds had to wait 35 years for a second FA Cup final, their first at Wembley. It's a personal disaster for Bob Paisley, dropped after scoring in the semi-final, and the afternoon ends in heartbreak as Liverpool lose to two goals from forward Reg Lewis.

3. Liverpool 2 Leeds United 1 1 May 1965
Finally, Liverpool get their hands on the FA Cup, but only after a titanic struggle over 120 minutes. Roger Hunt broke the deadlock three minutes into extra time, Leeds equalised through Billy Bremner, but Ian St John secured the silverware with nine minutes remaining.

4. Liverpool 1 Arsenal 2 8 May 1971
Despair for Liverpool after two hours of football as the Reds, in thick shirts on a blazing afternoon, failed to cope with the conditions. Eddie Kelly put Arsenal in front (although George Graham is still claiming it), Steve Heighway levelled before Charlie George famously let fly from 20 yards and celebrating flat on his back.

5. Liverpool 3 Newcastle United 0 4 May 1974
Pass and move at its finest in Shankly's curtain call as manager, silencing the pre-match boasts of Supermac's supermouth. Keegan got two, Heighway the other, and it could have been four if Alec Lindsay's goal hadn't been chalked off for offside. And there was an impressive display of velvet suits at the post-match banquet too.

6. Liverpool 1 Manchester United 2 21 May 1977
The missing link of the 1977 Treble bid – not even Terry McDermott's Kermit mascot could stop Tommy Docherty getting his hands on the Cup.

7. Liverpool 3 Everton 1 10 May 1986
How shall we count the ways the first Merseyside FA Cup final lives in the memory? Lineker outpacing Hansen to net the first-half opener is best forgotten, but Brucie's gymnastics in denying Sharp – and his spat with Beglin – were the prelude to an emphatic Red revival. Rushie's delicately arcing third goal ensured the Duchess of Kent, that alleged Liverpool fan, handed the trophy to Alan Hansen.

8. Liverpool 0 Wimbledon 1 14 May 1988
The biggest shock in over a century of FA Cup finals, as Bobby Gould's crazy gang overpowered the runaway champions. Beardsley had a beautifully chipped goal wrongly ruled out early on, before Lawrie Sanchez glanced a free kick beyond Grobbelaar and Dave Beasant saved the first penalty in a Wembley Cup final.

9. Liverpool 3 Everton 2 20 May 1989
The Hillsborough Cup final. *You'll Never Walk Alone* had only just drowned out the national anthem before Aldridge blasted home. It remained 1-0 for the next 86 minutes at which point Stuart McCall picked up on some tired defending and equalised. Ian Rush put Liverpool back in front during extra time, but McCall volleyed home a second equaliser – only for Rush to put the Reds back in front almost immediately with a deft header from a Barnes cross. Emotional.

10. Liverpool 2 Sunderland 0 9 May 1992
Ronnie Moran led out the Reds at Wembley as Graeme Souness, still recuperating from his heart operation, was accompanied on the bench by his doctor. Michael Thomas's spectacular scissor-kick put the Reds in front two minutes into the second-half, and Ian Rush scored his fifth goal in FA Cup finals. "You beauty!" yelled skipper Mark Wright as he lifted the Cup… or words to that effect.

11. Liverpool 2 Arsenal 1 12 May 2001
The first FA Cup final played outside Wembley in 80 years. Freddie Ljungberg looked to have buried a misfiring Liverpool on a scorching afternoon – until Michael Owen pounced on a Gary McAllister free kick with eight minutes left, and Patrik Berger launched a pin-point pass for Owen to run onto and fire past Seaman.

11. FIRST-EVER LIVERPOOL XI 1892

Ross

Hannah   McLean   McQue

Pearson McBride Wyllie Smith McVean

Cameron   Kelvin

The first ever Liverpool team got off to a sparkling start beating Higher Walton 8-0 in the Lancashire League 3 in September 1892.

FAMOUS FANS

Stars seen in the stands

1. **Nelson Mandela**
2. **Pope John Paul II**
3. **Cherie Blair**
4. **Samuel L Jackson**
5. **Mike Myers**
6. **Angelina Jolie and son Maddox**
7. **Jodie Kidd**
8. **Miss World Rosanna Davidson**
9. **Cilla Black**
10. **Ricky Tomlinson**
11. **Jimmy McGovern**

FANCY DRESS

11 costumes worn by Liverpool players at the Christmas party

1. **The Joker** Bruce Grobbelaar
2. **Ku Klux Klan member** John Barnes
3. **Beefeater** Ian Rush
4. **The Devil** Ronnie Whelan
5. **Luciano Pavarotti** Neil Ruddock
6. **Roman centurion** Jan Molby
7. **Nazi officer** Mark Wright
8. **Batman** Jamie Redknapp
9. **Robin** Don Hutchison
10. **Mickey Mouse** Steve Staunton
11. **Hunchback of Notre Dame** Jamie Carragher

FAR-FLUNG FAN CLUBS

11 supporters clubs from Accra to Velingrad

1. Accra, Ghana
2. Baku, Azerbaijan
3. Cape Town, South Africa
4. Dunedin, New Zealand
5. Lusaka, Zambia
6. Molde, Norway
7. Perth, Australia
8. Reykjavik, Iceland
9. Shanghai, China
10. Torshavn, Faroe Islands
11. Velingrad, Bulgaria

FIRST AND FOREMOST

11 records they can never take away

1. First club to win every home match in a season (1893/94)
2. First club to play in front of a reigning monarch (1914)
3. First club to win the league using just 14 players (1966)

11. FIRST EUROPEAN MATCH

Lawrence

Yeats   Moran   Byrne

Callaghan Milne Stevenson Wallace Thompson

Hunt   Chisnall

Liverpool's first steps on the road to an illustrious European record came against Reykjavik in the European Cup on 17 August 1964. The Reds won 5-0.

4. First club from England to beat Barcelona at home (1976)
5. First club to supply six players for a post-war England international (1977)
6. First club to concede just four goals at home in one league season (1978/79)
7. First club to have eight different players score in a match (1989)
8. First club in the league to have a shirt sponsor (1979)
9. First club to lift the FA Cup without an Englishman in the team (1986)
10. First club to win an FA Cup semi-final on penalties (1992)
11. First club to win a European final with a golden goal (2001)

FIRST FA CUP GAMES

Those first 11 steps on the road to Cup glory. "Bring on the Nantwich!"

1. Nantwich Town 0 Liverpool 4 preliminary round, 15 October 1892
2. Liverpool 9 Newtown 0 second qualifier, 29 October 1892
3. Northwich Victoria 2 Liverpool 1 third qualifier, 19 November 1892
4. Liverpool 3 Grimsby Town 0 first round, 27 January 1894
5. Liverpool 3 Preston North End 2 second round, 10 February 1894

6. **Bolton Wanderers 3 Liverpool 0** third round, 24 February 1894
7. **Barnsley St Peters 1 Liverpool 1** first round, 2 February 1895
8. **Liverpool 4 Barnsley St Peters 0** first round replay, 11 February 1895
9. **Liverpool 0 Nottingham Forest 2** second round, 16 February 1895
10. **Liverpool 4 Millwall 1** first round, 1 February 1896
11. **Wolverhampton Wanderers 2 Liverpool 0** second round, 15 February 1896

FIRST LEAGUE MATCHES

From the days when Arsenal still played at Woolwich

1. **Middlesbrough Ironopolis 0 Liverpool 2** 2 September 1893
2. **Liverpool 4 Lincoln City 0** 9 September 1893
3. **Ardwick 0 Liverpool 1** 16 September 1893
4. **Liverpool 3 Small Heath 1** 23 September 1893
5. **Notts County 1 Liverpool 1** 30 September 1893
6. **Liverpool 6 Middlesbrough Ironopolis 0** 7 October 1893
7. **Small Heath 3 Liverpool 4** 14 October 1893
8. **Burton Swifts 1 Liverpool 1** 21 October 1893
9. **Woolwich Arsenal 0 Liverpool 5** 28 October 1893
10. **Liverpool 5 Newcastle 1** 4 November 1893
11. **Walsall Town Swifts 1 Liverpool 1** 11 November 1893

FIRST MANAGERS

From Honest John to Shanks, the bosses who built Liverpool into a legend

1. John McKenna 1892-96
"Honest" John was a former grocer's errand boy turned freemason who effectively became the club's first manager. He assembled the "Team Of Macs" comprised entirely of Scots and Irishmen, guiding the club first into the Football League and then into the First Division.

2. William Barclay 1892-96
Officially, Barclay shared managerial duties with McKenna, although Barclay largely concentrated on the administrative side of the job. He later became headmaster of a school in Everton Crescent.

3. Tom Watson 1896-1915

Previously manager at Sunderland, Watson brought two championships to the club he oversaw from his house at 246 Anfield Road. He encouraged players and officials to enlist at the outbreak of the war and sent balls to the soldiers in the trenches.

4. David Ashworth 1920-23

Previously a referee, Ashworth boasted an impressive waxed moustache and led the Reds to the championship in 1922. Bizarrely, the following season he left the club, then top of the table, to take over at his old side Oldham, then bottom of it.

5. Matt McQueen 1923-28

Liverpool's next manager (one of the Team Of Macs) lived at 32 Kemlyn Road and secured the 1923 championship shortly after replacing Ashworth. He lost a leg in a road accident during a scouting mission, and retired in 1928.

6. George Patterson 1928-36

Patterson was unable to repeat the success of his predecessors, guiding the club to several mid-table finishes, although he did establish the tradition of nurturing home-grown talent and shrewd dealings in the transfer market, bringing Matt Busby and Phil Taylor to the club.

7. George Kay 1936-51

Kay arrived at the club from the manager's office at Southampton, having previously played for Bolton, appearing in the White Horse FA Cup final in 1923. He took the Reds to the league championship in 1947, having prepared his team on thick steaks in the sunshine of the USA before the season began.

8. Don Welsh 1951-56

Welsh was in charge when the team, hampered by an ageing attack, was relegated in 1954. Having spent big money on new players, he failed to steer the club back into the top flight and became the first Liverpool manager to be sacked.

9. Phil Taylor 1956-59

Having starred for Liverpool in 345 matches, Taylor seemed the ideal choice to lead the club back into Division One. However, too many near-misses in the promotion race and a humiliating FA Cup defeat to non-league Worcester City forced his resignation in 1959, having never managed the Reds in the top flight.

10. Bill Shankly 1959-74

Formerly a talented wing-half for Preston, Shankly moved into management at

Carlisle, and then had spells at Grimsby, Workington Town and Huddersfield Town. In 1959, chairman T.V. Williams decided Shankly was the man to take the club back into the big time. He was right. After a glorious career, however, Shankly's shock decision to resign, on 12 July 1974, has never been satisfactorily explained.

11. Bob Paisley 1974-83
For someone who said he never wanted the job anyway, the former brickie and desert rat made a pretty good fist of it: his record of three European Cups and six league championships is unlikely to be surpassed. In 1985 he was appointed adviser to Kenny Dalglish when the latter became the club's first player-manager.

FLAIR PLAYERS
Tricky wingers, visionary midfielders, space explorers and creative wizards

1. Peter Thompson
The right-footer illuminated the Liverpool left-wing in the 1960s after joining from Preston in 1963. Blessed with immaculate ball control, he flew down the flanks, collecting two championship medals and an FA Cup along the way. He might have won more than 16 England caps had Alf Ramsay not dispensed with wingers.

2. Steve Heighway
The economics graduate joined in 1970 from non-league Skelmersdale United. A right-winger in the No.9 shirt, he made an immediate impact with his electrifying runs, swerving past defenders and crossing with mathematical accuracy. Heighway made his debut for Ireland before he'd even appeared for Liverpool.

3. Terry McDermott
Terry Mac added the technique to perhaps the best midfield English football has ever seen, making key passes and his trademark deep penetrating runs into space, and scored more than his share of spectacular goals. The 'tache, the sovereign rings, the perm and the Bob Paisley impression lit up Anfield in the late 1970s.

4. Ray Kennedy
Bob Paisley converted Kennedy from a centre-forward into a sublime left-sided midfielder, creating countless goals with his intelligent runs and scoring. Now ill with Parkinson's disease, the Geordie is an all-time Liverpool legend.

5. Paul Walsh
Recruited from Luton Town in 1984. Injuries and the presence of Dalglish and Rush meant that he never quite established himself at Anfield but his skill, pace and ability to wriggle out of the tightest situations made him a playground icon. Scored a hat-trick against Norwich with a plastercast on his arm.

6. Jan Molby
The Dane could unlock a match with one sublime pass, his performance in the 1986 FA Cup final perhaps being the perfect illustration of his talents. He had a forceful shot and took a mean penalty too. Injury, weight problems and a prison sentence conspired against him but he remains one of the mostly fondly remembered Reds.

7. Peter Beardsley
Supplied the guile, wizardry and some deftly shimmying hips to the frontline after Dalglish retired, linking up superbly with Barnes and Aldridge in the majestic 1987/88 team. But he departed Anfield all too prematurely.

8. Steve McManaman
Macca was a teenage Everton fan but signed for Liverpool, enticed by a pair of rare Puma boots given to him by Kenny Dalglish. It was Goodison's loss as his roaming, loping style split defences and fashioned innumerable goals for his team-mates.

9. Patrik Berger
He sometimes flattered to deceive, but had few Premiership peers on his day. Two goals against Chelsea in his first start for the Reds, a surface-to-air rocket against Derby and a pinpoint crossfield ball to set up Michael Owen's winner against Arsenal in the 2001 FA Cup final are etched into the memory forever.

10. Jari Litmanen
The enigmatic Finn ought to have become a Red legend but after signing him from Barcelona in 2001, Gerard Houllier under-used the skilful forward whose highlights include a beauty against Bayer Leverkusen and a magical Cruyff turn against Spurs.

11. Xabi Alonso
The deft midfielder was handed his chance as a 19-year-old at Real Sociedad by John Toshack before joining Liverpool for £10.7m in 2004. Dubbed a "slim Jan Molby", the Spanish international possesses the same vision and range of passing.

FOOTBALLERS OF THE YEAR

Selected by their peers and the press

1. Ian Callaghan FWA Footballer of the Year 1974
2. Kevin Keegan FWA Footballer of the Year 1976
3. Emlyn Hughes FWA Footballer of the Year 1977
4. Kenny Dalglish FWA Footballer of the Year 1979, 1983; PFA Player of the Year 1983
5. Terry McDermott FWA Footballer of the Year 1980; PFA Player of the Year 1980
6. Ian Rush PFA Young Player of the Year 1983; FWA and PFA Player of the Year 1984
7. John Barnes FWA Footballer of the Year 1988, 1990; PFA Player of the Year 1988
8. Steve Nicol FWA Footballer of the Year 1989
9. Robbie Fowler PFA Young Player of the Year 1995, 1996
10. Michael Owen PFA Young Player of the Year 1998; France Football European Footballer of the Year 2001
11. Steven Gerrard PFA Young Player of the Year 2001

GOAL HAULS

11 players who earned the match ball... but didn't stop there

1. J. Miller scored five against Fleetwood Rovers, 1892
His first name remains a mystery but what isn't in doubt is the fact he scored five goals in one game during Liverpool's inaugural season.

2. Andy McGuigan five against Stoke City, 1902
The Scot became the first Liverpool player to score five goals in a football league match, in a 7-0 defeat of Stoke in January 1902.

3. Ian Rush five against Luton Town, 1983
During his untouchable 1983/84 season, Rush netted five in a 6-0 rout. Remarkably, Tony Woodcock also performed the same feat for Arsenal on the same afternoon.

4. John Evans five against Bristol Rovers, 1954
Evans went nap in Liverpool's 5-3 defeat of Rovers, later scoring four at Bury.

5. Robbie Fowler five against Fulham, 1993
Fowler announced his arrival as Rush's heir by going nap in a League Cup tie at Anfield in just his fourth start for the first team.

6. Fred Howe four against Everton, 1935
Ian Rush wasn't the first Liverpool player to score four goals against the Blues. In September 1935, the forward pulled off the achievement in a 6-0 thrashing.

7. Billy Liddell four against Ipswich Town, 1954
On Christmas Day 1954, Liddell delivered four goals for the Anfield faithful, one from the spot, in a 6-2 romp against Ipswich.

8. Roger Hunt four against Stoke City, 1963
Nine years on, Sir Roger got in the festive spirit by nabbing four goals in a 6-1 Boxing Day hiding of Stoke at Anfield.

9. Ian Rush four against Everton, 1982
6 November 1982 is still commemorated in song at Anfield, as Rush mercilessly dismantled the Blues's defence to score four in a 5-0 rout at Goodison Park.

10. Dean Saunders four against Kuusysi Lahti, 1991
Saunders became the first Liverpool player to score four goals in a European match on the club's return to continental competition, against the Finnish minnows.

11. Robbie Fowler four against Middlesbrough, 1996
Fowler checked an imaginary watch after scoring the first in 30 seconds, revealed his "God's job's a good 'un" T-shirt after the second (his 100th for the club), raised a pitchside mic in triumph on the third and stuck the ball up his shirt on the final whistle, having made it four.

GOALKEEPING UNDERSTUDIES

11 number two number ones

1. Steve Ogrizovic
Big Oggy arrived from Chesterfield in 1977, but as he ranked behind Ray Clemence

he only saw first-team action on five occasions. He later moved to Shrewsbury and Coventry, where he became a legend appearing in 601 matches. Hoaxers recently claimed he had been kidnapped in Kazakhstan.

2. Bob Wardle
The Shrewsbury keeper arrived at Anfield in 1982 in an exchange deal involving Ogrizovic, but could never dislodge Grobbelaar from the No.1 shirt.

3. Bob Bolder
Bolder joined Liverpool for £125,000 from Sheffield Wednesday in 1983, but never made a first-team appearance due to Bruce Grobbelaar's remarkable consistency.

4. Chris Pile
The 18-year-old Pile was on the bench for the 1985 European Cup final in the absence of the injured Bolder, but never appeared for the first team.

5. Mike Hooper
The man with a degree in English literature made 73 appearances for the Reds over seven years, but was never truly first choice. He joined the club in 1985 from Wrexham for £40,000, making his debut in the following year's Charity Shield.

6. Tony Warner
Nicknamed Tony Bonus by Robbie Fowler, after sitting on the Liverpool bench 120 times and duly picking up more than a few win bonuses, but Warner never tasted first-team football at the club.

7. Michael Stensgaard
The Danish U21 international never played a first-team game for Liverpool, and an infamous shoulder injury sustained in a freak ironing-board incident brought a premature end to a promising career.

8. Jorgen Nielsen
Nielsen was another Dane who never quite managed to make the breakthrough, despite sitting on the bench in more than 50 Premiership matches.

9. Pegguy Arphexad
Guadeloupe-born Arphexad joined Liverpool from Leicester City in 1999 as back-up to Sander Westerveld, and made six appearances in four seasons at the club, only two of those coming in the Premiership.

10. Patrice Luzi
The Frenchman's only taste of first-team action came as a 77th-minute substitute for the injured Jerzy Dudek in a 1-0 victory at Chelsea in 2004.

11. Paul Jones
The Welshman and boyhood Red jumped at the chance to join the club for two appearances in 2004, when Dudek and Chris Kirkland were injured.

GOAL RUSH

He scored more than 300 times for the Reds. Here are 11 of Ian's finest

1. The arcing, camera-busting third versus Everton in the 1986 FA Cup final
2. The first-time, left-footed volley at Villa Park in 1984
3. The surge, feint and finish for his fourth against Everton in 1982
4. The deft chip over the Dynamo Bucharest goalkeeper in 1984
5. The deft glancing header to win the 1989 FA Cup final against Everton
6. The hat-trick in the rain against Benfica in the 1983/84 European Cup
7. The last-minute finish at a frozen White Hart Lane in March 1986
8. The turn and rifled shot into the roof of the net at Watford in 1986
9. The rebound tucked away to deny Manchester United the title in 1992
10. The downward header beyond the keeper at Atletico Bilbao in November 1983
11. The simple sidefoot to secure the FA Cup against Sunderland in 1992

GOOD FRIDAYS... AND MONDAYS

11 memorable Easter fixtures

1. Liverpool 2 Chelsea 0 19 April 1965
The Reds had lost 4-0 at Stamford Bridge on Good Friday, but goals from Phil Chisnall and Geoff Strong earned back their respect on Easter Monday.

2. Manchester United 0 Liverpool 3 3 April 1972
Strikes from Chris Lawler, John Toshack and Emlyn Hughes completed an Easter Monday rout of the Mancs in front of 54,000 fans at Old Trafford.

3. Liverpool 2 Leeds United 0 23 April 1973
Cormack and Keegan are the marksmen for Liverpool in defeat of Don Revie's side.

4. Manchester City 0 Liverpool 3 19 April 1976
This Easter Monday fixture had remained deadlocked until Steve Heighway netted in the 73rd minute. Two in a minute from David Fairclough sealed the win late on.

5. Manchester City 0 Liverpool 4 4 April 1983
Fairclough repeated his feat of seven years earlier, scoring twice in an Easter Monday romp at Maine Road. Graeme Souness and Alan Kennedy were also on the mark.

6. Liverpool 2 Manchester City 0 31 March 1986
Liverpool stepped up a gear in the title race, two goals from Steve McMahon in another Easter Monday defeat of City putting the pressure on Everton.

7. Liverpool 3 Manchester United 3 4 April 1988
The mighty Reds were 3-1 up on Easter Monday before throwing away their lead. Cue Strachan's cigar in front of the Kop and a domestic involving Kenny and Fergie.

8. Tottenham Hotspur 1 Liverpool 2 26 March 1989
John Aldridge's penalty and a Peter Beardsley strike collected the points at White Hart Lane in a rare Easter Sunday fixture.

9. Liverpool 2 West Ham United 0 8 April 1996
Liverpool's Premiership challenge had faltered after defeat at Coventry on the Saturday, but two days later Collymore and Barnes earned three points at Anfield.

10. Manchester United 1 Liverpool 1 10 April 1998
Michael Owen received his marching orders in this stormy Good Friday clash, having equalised for the Reds just four minutes earlier.

11. Everton 0 Liverpool 0 21 April 2000
This Good Friday derby is best remembered for the disallowed last-second 'winner' that bounced off Don Hutchison's backside from Westerveld's free kick.

GREAT DEFENDERS

11 touch tacklers, dashing full-backs and cool liberos

1. Chris Lawler
The Silent Knight effortlessly patrolled the right-back spot with a minimum of fuss between 1962 and 1975, rarely missing a game and frequently popping up in the

opposition's penalty area to round off a move, scoring 61 goals in 549 appearances.

> **FAIRCLOUGH REPEATED HIS FEAT... SCORING TWICE IN A 4-0 EASTER MONDAY ROMP AT MAINE ROAD**

2. Gerry Byrne
Best remembered for playing practically the entire 1965 FA Cup final with a broken collarbone, Byrne could play at right-back as well as on his usual left. He could read a game with assurance, but had a fearsome challenge as well, and once broke Tommy Smith's nose on the training field.

3. Emlyn Hughes
Hughes joined Liverpool as a midfielder, moving back into the Reds' defence in 1973 when he teamed up with Phil Thompson. Blessed with inexhaustible stamina, he frequently made effective surges into the opposition penalty area and was dubbed Crazy Horse after felling one Newcastle forward with a rugby tackle.

4. Phil Neal
Zico played 417 consecutive matches for Liverpool from 1974 to 1983, a model of consistency that is unlikely to be beaten. He wasn't the toughest tackler, preferring to use his intelligence to deny an attacker space or jockeying them into giving the ball away, but he scored 59 goals, many of them coolly dispatched from the spot.

5. Alan Kennedy
Barney Rubble had an uncompromising tackle, a talent for making buccaneering runs and a powerful if erratic left-footed shot, which once knocked off a policeman's helmet. He was signed from Newcastle United by Bob Paisley, who used to buy fish and chips from Kennedy's mother.

6. Phil Thompson
Kirkby's favourite son might have had the legs of a sparrow when he first broke into the first team but he rapidly proved himself with a rare blend of tough tackling and assuredness, eventually assuming the team captaincy. His poise earned him 42 caps for England, excelling at the 1982 World Cup.

7. Alan Hansen
Perhaps the closest thing to a continental libero that British football has ever seen, Jocky brought panache, elegance and a distaste for breaking sweat to Liverpool's defence. He could bring the ball out like Beckenbauer and preferred brain to brawn, rarely being dumped on his backside. Pure class.

8. Steve Nicol

He took size 13 boots and had a habit of being repeatedly caught out by practical jokes, but Chico was one of the most dedicated defenders Anfield has ever seen. The Scot filled every position in the back four at some point and excelled in all of them.

9. Steve Staunton

The composed left-back clocked up 147 appearances in two separate spells at Anfield. Recruited from Dundalk by Kenny Dalglish in 1986, he was assured on the ball, a good distributor and a dangerous raider. He even netted a hat-trick as an emergency forward in a League Cup tie against Wigan Athletic.

10. Rob Jones

Graeme Souness signed the right-back from Crewe in October 1991. Forty-eight hours later he was playing a blinder in a live TV match against Manchester United, effortlessly shackling Ryan Giggs. Five months later he was playing for England. He linked up superbly with McManaman, but injuries stalled, then ended, his career.

11. Sami Hyypia

The Finn has become the heart of the Reds' defence since arriving from Holland's Willem II in 1999. Sami has the kind of neck that seems to extend in an aerial duel, plus a formidable presence and an impressive knack for reading the game.

GREATEST GOALKEEPERS

The most reliable gloves in the business: Liverpool's 11 finest No.1s

1. Harry Storer

The first Liverpool goalkeeper to make the jersey his own, Storer made 121 appearances between 1895-1900, helping the Reds to promotion in 1896 and establishing the best defensive record in the top flight in 1898/99.

2. Teddy Doig

One of the most respected keepers of his generation, the Scottish international's prime had come at Sunderland before he joined Liverpool in 1904. His saves helped the club to promotion in his first season, and happily he never repeated his mistake on Wearside of conceding a goal direct from the opposing keeper's goal kick.

3. Sam Hardy

The England international kept goal for Liverpool for seven seasons, having joined

from Chesterfield in 1905 for £500. Like so many of his successors, Hardy wasn't a spectacular keeper, preferring to rely on uncanny anticipation to deny forwards.

4. Elisha Scott
He stood just 5ft 9 1/2in, but it scarcely mattered, as the Irishman had "the eye of an eagle, the swift movement of a panther and the clutch of a vice" according to one reporter. A spectacular save against Blackburn prompted one supporter to run on the pitch and kiss Scott… and this was in 1924. Liverpool once accepted a bid from Everton to buy him but a newspaper campaign by fans changed their minds. There were tears on the Kop the day he decided to retire back to Belfast.

5. Arthur Riley
Like Grobbelaar, Riley was born in South Africa, making 338 appearances between 1925 and 1940. He had the task of filling Scott's gloves, and never quite emulated his predecessor's impregnable aura, but for longevity his contribution deserves applause.

6. Cyril Sidlow
One of the first to throw the ball to a team-mate rather than kicking it, Liverpool's first post-war goalkeeper hailed from Colwyn Bay. Suffered from occasional lapses in concentration, but helped the Reds to the league championship in 1947, his finest hour perhaps coming in a 2-1 victory over his former club and title rivals Wolves.

7. Tommy Younger
The colossal Scottish international commanded his six-yard area, and his 15-stone frame meant any forceful opposition forwards had problems. He once went off injured and came back on as centre-forward. He made 120 appearances.

8. Tommy Lawrence
The Flying Pig joined Liverpool in 1957 but the agile Scot didn't actually make his debut until 1962. He made up for it, missing just four games in six successful seasons. Lawrence was also dubbed the Sweeper Keeper for his habit of coming off his line to tidy up danger. In 1968/69 he conceded just 24 goals, then a record.

9. Ray Clemence
The former deckchair attendant from Skegness cost Liverpool a mere £18,000 from Scunthorpe in 1967, but his agility and astute positioning proved priceless during the 1970s. In 1978/79 he beat Lawrence's record by conceding just 16 goals. In 1981 he joined Tottenham, and the picture of him and the Kop applauding each other on his return the following season remains one of the iconic Anfield images.

10. Bruce Grobbelaar

His name has been tainted by headlines and covert video footage, but that doesn't detract from the former soldier's gymnastic saves and dazzling showmanship during the 1980s. He made mistakes, but they were outweighed by an enviable record in the "goals against" ledger, and those spaghetti legs in Rome aren't likely to be forgotten.

11. Jerzy Dudek

The big Pole has had some moments to forget since joining, but his performance in the Champions League final earned him an indelible place in Anfield lore. First a Banks-like double save from Andriy Shevchenko in the dying minutes of extra time, before his antics won the cup for Liverpool. Dudek dedicated his medal to the late Pope John Paul II, who had told him he was a fan of the goalkeeper and the Reds.

HAIRDOS AND DON'TS

Mop-tops, mullets and perms. The players who turned on the style for the Reds

1. Terry McDermott

He reckoned it was in the "top ten of British perms, alongside Leo Sayer."

2. Barry Venison

The classic mid-1980s blond "short on the top and leave it long at the back" look.

3. Craig Johnston
Skippy boasted a fulsome head of ringlets throughout the 1980s.

4. Robbie Fowler
In 1995, God briefly opted for the bleached-blond image.

5. Peter Beardsley

The touch was always immaculate, the pudding-bowl haircut rather less so.

6. Abel Xavier
Bleached hair and matching beard were distinctive to say the least.

7. Patrik Berger
Forget the Alice band – Paddy's flowing locks were made for electrifying runs.

8. Alun Evans The Kop's very own 1960s mop-top.

9. Steve McManaman
Shaggy's tousled locks perfectly suited his entertaining style of play.

10. Anthony Le Tallec
The French gem sported a blinding blond look in the summer of 2004.

11. Gary McAllister He had no hair. But we didn't care.

HARD MEN

11 Reds only the most foolhardy dared tangle with

1. Tommy Smith
The Anfield Iron was one of the toughest defenders English football has ever seen,
an aggressive ball-winner who could, as the cliché has it, play a bit too.

2. Ron Yeats
The Colossus was the rock on which Liverpool's success was founded. Thunderous in
the challenge, the former slaughterman stood 6ft 2in and was indomitable in the air.
He captained the team for ten years.

3. Larry Lloyd
Dominant in the air, and possessing a powerful tackle and remarkable sideburns,
Larry Valentine Lloyd made 218 appearances over five seasons at Anfield before
moving on to Nottingham Forest.

4. Joey Jones
The indomitable Welshman regularly menaced opponents after joining in 1975
from Wrexham. Steely tackle, strong in the air and with a never-say-die attitude.

5. Graeme Souness
Fearless in the Liverpool engine room, Souness had a tungsten tackle shrouded in
silk. His bite memorably transformed a game at Spurs in 1982 after coming on as
substitute following an injury, inspiring the Reds from 2-0 down to a 2-2 draw.

6. Jimmy Case
The former apprentice electrician brought fierce determination and a ferocious tackle to the late-1970s midfield, after joining from South Liverpool in 1972.

7. Steve McMahon
Never took prisoners during his reign in the midfield from 1985 to 1991, relishing a succession of bone-crunching derby duels with Everton counterpart Peter Reid.

8. Neil Ruddock
The importance of Razor was underlined when he was dropped for the 1996 FA Cup final and was sorely missed. He memorably tangled with Eric Cantona, repeatedly turning down the Frenchman's collar, goading him into earning a yellow card.

9. Paul Ince
Reviled by Reds when he played for Manchester United, the self-styled Guv'nor never quite recaptured that imperious form when he joined Liverpool from Inter in 1997, although he did score a memorable last-gasp equaliser against United in 1999.

10. Steven Gerrard
It's amazing to think that in their academy days, Gerrard was the same height as Michael Owen. He has emerged as an extraordinary midfield presence, relishing his battles with Keane and Vieira and promising to reach the same heights as Souness.

11. Jamie Carragher
Scouse and sound, as the chant goes, Carra is a defender of class and distinction, one blessed with the full-blooded enthusiasm of a Jones and the passion of a Smith.

HAT-TRICK HEAVEN
The deadly legends who made it look as easy as 1-2-3

1. Albert Stubbins Liverpool 4 Birmingham City 1, 1 March 1947
The legend's treble in this FA Cup quarter-final on a freezing afternoon included a memorable second that became known as the "goal in the snow". Billy Liddell crossed hard and low from the left and Stubbins launched into a remarkable diving header which flew into the top corner of the net.

2. Roger Hunt Tottenham Hotspur 1 Liverpool 3, 27 March 1964
Sir Roger enjoyed one very Good Friday during Liverpool's first championship

season for 17 years. He effortlessly struck two past Spurs keeper John Hollowbread at White Hart Lane before earning the match ball with a header 20 minutes from time.

3. Alun Evans Liverpool 3 Bayern Munich 1, 3 November 1971
Evans single-handedly destroyed Franz Beckenbauer and co in this Inter-Cities Fairs Cup quarter-final at Anfield. His inch-prefect first strike left Sepp Maier grasping for air and earned Evans the goal of the month award from *Match Of The Day*. It was Liverpool's first-ever hat-trick in Europe.

4. Graeme Souness Liverpool 5 CSKA Sofia 1, 4 March 1981
The imperious Scot demolished the Bulgarian champions in a European Cup quarter-final, including a screamer into the Kop net for the third. Cue Barry Davies: "Souness! What a way to complete a hat-trick! The keeper didn't even see it!"

5. Ian Rush Aston Villa 1 Liverpool 3, 20 January 1984
Masterly finishing from the ruthless assassin in front of the BBC's live cameras on a frosty Friday night at Villa Park. Rush's second-half treble erased a first-half deficit, the best was an audacious chip over the head of 6ft 3in Nigel Spink for his third.

6. Jan Molby Liverpool 3 Coventry City 1, 26 November 1986
Rambo netted the club's only hat-trick of penalties in a Littlewoods Cup fourth-round replay in November 1986, netting on four, 39 and 72 minutes. Point of fact: this was the first Liverpool match attended by future Reds captain Steven Gerrard.

7. Steve Nicol Newcastle United 1 Liverpool 4, 20 September 1987
In the opening weeks of the 1987/88 season, Chico embarked on an improbable scoring run, climaxed by this Sunday afternoon treble screened live on the BBC. The third was the best, Nicol racing down the right wing and chipping Alan Kelly, putting Newcastle's new Brazilian striker Mirandinha in the shade.

8. Ronnie Rosenthal Charlton Athletic 0 Liverpool 4, 11 April 1990
Days after a dispiriting FA Cup 4-3 defeat to Crystal Palace, Liverpool's new on-loan striker put the team's title challenge back on track with a perfect hat-trick – one with his left foot, one with his right and the third with his head. Rosenthal was the first Liverpool player to score a hat trick on his debut in 26 years.

9. Peter Beardsley Liverpool 4 Manchester United 0, 16 September 1990
United keeper Les Sealey was so sick of the sight of Beardsley after this hat-trick, he booted the match ball into the Kop.

10. Robbie Fowler Liverpool 3 Arsenal 0, 28 August 1994
It took Fowler just four minutes and 33 seconds to make Premiership history. The first was poached from eight yards out, the second followed a deft counterattack involving Redknapp and McManaman, and the third came from the rebound following a save by the hapless David Seaman.

11. Michael Owen Newcastle United 1 Liverpool 4, 30 August 1998
Enter Ruud Gullit. It was meant to be the Newcastle manager's day, but nobody told Owen as he ripped the Magpies's defence apart. Everybody remembers the third, as he outpaced Philippe Albert to a through ball and beat Shay Given.

HEAVIEST DEFEATS

If you don't want to know the results, look away now

1. **Birmingham City 9 Liverpool 1** Division Two, 11 December 1954
2. **Huddersfield Town 8 Liverpool 0** Division One, 10 November 1934
3. **Newcastle United 9 Liverpool 2** Division One, 1 January 1934
4. **Bolton Wanderers 8 Liverpool 1** Division One, 7 May 1932
5. **Arsenal 8 Liverpool 1** Division One, 1 September 1934
6. **Sunderland 7 Liverpool 0** Division One, 7 December 1912
7. **West Ham United 7 Liverpool 0** Division One, 1 September 1930
8. **Arsenal 6 Liverpool 0** Division One, 28 November 1931
9. **Manchester City 6 Liverpool 0** Division One, 11 September 1935
10. **Charlton Athletic 6 Liverpool 0** Division One, 26 September 1953
11. **Liverpool 0 Sunderland 6** Division One, 19 April 1930 – record home defeat

HIGHEST PREMIERSHIP SHIRT NUMBERS

"France's, France's number 39, France's number 39"

1. **39** Patrice Luzi
2. **37** Jari Litmanen
3. **36** Jon Otsemobor
4. **34** Darren Potter
5. **33** Neil Mellor
6. **32** Jon Newby
7. **32** John Welsh

8. 31 David Raven
9. 30 Djimi Traore
10. 29 Brad Friedel
11. 29 Stephen Wright

INCREDIBLE JOHN BARNES MOMENTS

When he did his thing, the crowd went bananas. Dig this…

1. The curling extra-time strike into the far corner in the 4-4 draw at Goodison in 1991.
2. The acrobatic scissor kick "for the scrapbook" at Blackburn Rovers in 1994.
3. The perfectly weighted cross for John Aldridge in the 1988 FA Cup semi-final.
4. The sublime right-footed backheel at Crewe in the 1992 FA Cup third round.
5. The stunning, arced free kick at home to Arsenal in 1989.
6. The floated cross for Ian Rush's second in the 1989 FA Cup final.
7. The dribble past three Forest defenders and pull-back for Peter Beardsley in 1988.
8. The looping headed goal at Aston Villa in the FA Cup in 1988.
9. The lay-off for Stan Collymore in the 4-3 against Newcastle United in 1996.
10. The run from the half-way line and finish against Manchester United in 1990.
11. The free kick against Portsmouth in the 1992 semi, bundled home by Whelan.

INTERNATIONALS AT ANFIELD

England and Scotland have felt at home before the Kop. Ireland and Wales less so

1. England 6 Ireland 1 home international, 1899
2. Wales 0 Scotland 2 World Cup qualifier, 1977
3. Holland 2 Ireland 0 Euro 96 play-off, 1995
4. Italy 2 Russia 1 Euro 96
5. Czech Republic 2 Italy 1 Euro 96
6. Czech Republic 3 Russia 3 Euro 96
7. France 0 Holland 0 Euro 96, France win on penalties

8. Italy 2 Wales 0 Euro 2000 qualifier, 1998
9. Denmark 2 Wales 0 Euro 2000 qualifier, 1999
10. England 2 Finland 1 World Cup qualifier, 2001
11. England 4 Paraguay 0 friendly 2001

IRISH REDS

11 Reds who represented the Emerald Isle… although not all hailed from there

1. Phil Babb Lambeth, London
2. Jim Beglin Waterford
3. Steve Finnan Limerick
4. Steve Heighway Dublin
5. Ray Houghton Glasgow
6. Mark Kennedy Dublin
7. Richie Partridge Dublin
8. Michael Robinson Leicester
9. Kevin Sheedy Builth Wells, Wales
10. Steve Staunton Drogheda
11. Ronnie Whelan Dublin

IT'S GOT OUR NAME ON IT

11 memorable encounters from the League Cup, the trophy we can't help winning

1. Manchester United 2-1, third round, 1985/86
Liverpool's bid for a fifth League Cup ultimately ended in defeat to Queen's Park Rangers at the semi-final stage but not before Dalglish's men had satisfyingly dumped Big Ron out of the competition in the third round. The match was lit up by an atomic-powered rocket from Jan Molby. "He won the ball from Whiteside, he ran 30 yards towards goal and he lashed it past Bailey into the back of the net!" as Peter Jones breathlessly exclaimed on Radio 2. Due to a contractual dispute over television coverage, only the 41,291 at Anfield that night ever saw it.

2. QPR 2-2, semi-final, 1985/86
Everybody remembers Liverpool won the Double in 1986, but not everyone recalls how close we came to doing a Treble that season. The Reds had lost the first leg 1-0 at Loftus Road, and contrived a bizarre draw in the return at Anfield, in which Gary

Gillespie and Ronnie Whelan netted own-goals and Jan Molby missed a penalty.

3. Fulham 10-0, second round, first leg, 1986/87
It remains Liverpool's biggest domestic victory, and if Steve McMahon hadn't missed a penalty it could have been more. Still, he did score four goals on the night so it seems a bit unfair to blame him. Two each from Ian Rush and John Wark, and strikes from Ronnie Whelan and Steve Nicol put Liverpool into double figures. The programme for the second leg at Craven Cottage reminded fans that, "If the scores are level after 90 minutes, extra time will be played."

4 Everton 1-0, fifth round, 1986/87
In the mid-1980s, it seemed like Liverpool were duelling with Everton for the highest stakes every few weeks. Unfortunately, this tight tie at Goodison Park is invariably remembered for the broken leg sustained by Jim Beglin in a challenge with Gary Stevens that effectively ended the Irishman's Liverpool career. It overshadowed the intervention of Alan Irvine, who came on to run the Blues's defence ragged before, inevitably, Ian Rush shattered Everton dreams in the 83rd minute. "It's the old, old story," as BBC commentator Barry Davies put it.

5. Arsenal 2-1, third round, second replay, 1988/89
It's been practically forgotten due to the more momentous match between these two clubs at the end of this season, but none of the 21,708 spectators on neutral territory at Villa Park is likely to forget this night. Three-and-a-half hours had failed to separate the two teams, but deprived of half a team through injury, including Barnes, Hansen and Grobbelaar, Liverpool's prospects didn't look great. Yet thanks to an electric atmosphere generated by the travelling Reds, and strikes from McMahon and Aldridge, Liverpool gave George Graham's prospective champions a footballing lesson. And Kenny Dalglish got hit by a packet of butties from the Arsenal fans, which he promptly returned.

6. Fulham 5-0, second round, second leg, 1993/94
Five good reasons to celebrate this match, all of them from the sanctified boots of Robbie Fowler. In just his fourth start for the Reds, he ended up sticking five past hapless Fulham goalkeeper Jim Stannard. That night there were just 12,541 fans inside Anfield to witness the birth of an Anfield legend as the 18-year-old became just the fifth Red to score five goals in one game.

7. Chelsea 2-1, League Cup, third round, 2000/01
Robbie Fowler settled this classic cup tie in extra time, after Gianfranco Zola had cancelled out Danny Murphy's 12th-minute opener. Emile Heskey was sent off just

seconds from the end for lashing out after a two-footed tackle from Marcel Desailly. There was even a half-time appearance from infamous streaker Mark Roberts, who jumped onto the pitch at the restart, nicked the ball off a bemused Zola before dribbling through the Chelsea players and shooting past Ed De Goey.

8. Stoke City 8-0, fourth round, 2000/01
Liverpool's record away victory was racked up at the Britannia Stadium in November 2000. Christian Ziege opened the rout on six minutes, while Vladimir Smicer, Markus Babbel, Sami Hyypia, Danny Murphy and a hat-trick from Robbie Fowler compounded the misery for the Potters.

9. Crystal Palace 5-0, semi-final, second leg, 2000/01
Proof, if the Kop needed it, that revenge is sweet. Liverpool had lost the first leg at Selhurst Park 2-1 to the Division One club, their striker Clinton Morrison declaring that he was in better scoring form than Michael Owen. In the second leg, however, the Reds swept the Eagles aside thanks to goals from Smicer, Biscan, Fowler and two from Murphy. Morrison's nose was rubbed in it when, presented with a glorious goalscoring opportunity in front of the Kop, he unleashed a complete airshot.

10. Aston Villa 4-3, fifth round, 2002/03
It didn't kick off until five past nine, thanks to a cock-up at the Villa Park ticket office, but this see-saw cup tie was just about worth waiting for on a freezing Birmingham evening. Darius Vassell put Villa ahead from the spot on 23 minutes, only for Danny Murphy, Milan Baros and Steven Gerrard to give Liverpool what looked like a commanding 3-1 lead. But Thomas Hitzlsperger pulled one back and Dion Dublin levelled six minutes from time, only for Murphy to snatch it back for the Reds.

11. Tottenham Hotspur 1-1, 5-4 on penalties, fifth round 2004/05
The night the Benitez babes dumped a full-strength Tottenham team out of the Carling Cup will live long in the memory, not least for an amazing atmosphere at the Liverpool end, and a 20-minute rendition of the Ra-ra-ra-rafa *La Bamba* song. Effectively fielding a youth team, albeit one strengthened by Jerzy Dudek and Stephane Henchoz, Liverpool held on for extra time, but didn't give up when Jermain Defoe put Spurs in front. Three minutes from the end, Kanoute handled in the area and Florent Sinama-Pongolle coolly converted the penalty. The youngsters triumphed 5-4 in the shoot-out, Flo hitting the winner, and took a well-deserved bow in front of the away fans.

KOP MOSAICS

11 matches preceded by a spot of community artistry from the Kop

1. **v Sheffield Wednesday 1998** Hillsborough
2. **v Coventry City 1999** Shankly day
3. **v Roma 2001** three European Cups – Bob Paisley night
4. **v Manchester United 2001** GH tricolore – get well Houllier
5. **v Roma 2002** Allez
6. **v Bayer Leverkusen 2002** red-and-white chequered flag

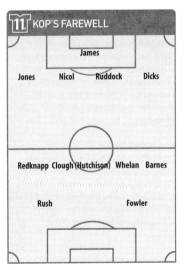

11. KOP'S FAREWELL

James

Jones   Nicol   Ruddock   Dicks

Redknapp   Clough (Hutchison)   Whelan   Barnes

Rush   Fowler

The final game before the Kop changed from a terrace to all-seater Kop grandstand was a 1-0 defeat to Norwich City on 30 April 1994.

7. v Ipswich Town 2002 YNWA MB – for Markus Babbel after debilitating illness
8. v Manchester United 2002 This Is Anfield
9. v Marseille 2003 Allez Allez
10. v Newcastle United 2004 tenth anniversary of Kop's last stand
11. v Olympiakos 2004 96+21 – for victims of Hillsborough and the Karaiskaki stadium tragedy of 1981, when 21 Greek fans lost their lives in a closed-gate crush

LEAGUE CUP FINALS

Seven wins, three defeats, a replay and a lot of classic moments

1. Nottingham Forest 0-0 and 0-1, 18 and 22 March 1978
Liverpool had never taken the League Cup seriously until the 1970s – indeed they had only reached the last eight twice prior to 1978, when they faced Brian Clough's ascendant Forest at Wembley. The first match ended goalless, with Liverpool unable to beat 18-year-old goalkeeper Chris Woods, who had replaced the cup-tied Peter Shilton. But it's for the Old Trafford replay four days later that this encounter is remembered, specifically Phil Thompson's foul on John O'Hare that earned Forest a penalty. Thommo rightly swore on his life it was outside the box, but John Robertson stuck away the spot-kick, leaving Phil with the consolation of bringing the phrase "professional foul" into the football lexicon.

2. West Ham United 1-1 and 2-1, 14 March and 6 April 1981
The first match against John Lyall's Hammers remained goalless for 118 minutes, until Alan Kennedy put the Reds in front, despite Sammy Lee lying on the pitch in an offside position. But Terry McDermott's last-minute handball earned West Ham a penalty which Ray Stewart converted. In the Villa Park replay, the Reds went behind to an early Paul Goddard strike, but goals from Kenny Dalglish and the head of Alan Hansen inside three minutes handed the Cup to Liverpool for the first time.

3. Tottenham Hotspur 3-1, 13 March 1982
Liverpool's reign as cup-holders appeared to be ending after Steve Archibald's

first-half goal and several impressive saves by Ray Clemence to deny his former team-mates. But with just three minutes left, Ronnie Whelan's equaliser forced extra time, and Bob Paisley urged his players to stay on their feet during the interval while Spurs rested on the turf. It did the psychological trick as Whelan struck again to give the Reds the lead, before Rush sealed it right at the end, stroking that weird red-and-white Sondico ball over the line.

4. Manchester United 2-1, 26 March 1983
For the second season running, the Reds had to come from behind to lift what had become the Milk Cup. Prodigious teenager Norman Whiteside had given United the lead before the interval, but with 15 minutes remaining Alan Kennedy hit an equaliser to send the final into extra time. United suffered, Frank Stapleton having to switch places with Gordon McQueen due to cramp. But Liverpool moved up another gear. Again Ronnie Whelan was the hero, curling an audacious winner into the top corner of Gary Bailey's net to make it a hat-trick of League Cups for the Reds. But perhaps the most enduring memory is that of Bob Paisley, reluctantly but deservedly ascending the Wembley steps to receive the trophy in his last final.

5. Everton 0-0, 25 March 1984
"Mer-sey-side, Mer-sey-side!" For the first time in a century of football, Liverpool and Everton met at Wembley, as Howard Kendall's resurgent Blues attempted to deny Joe Fagan's team their fourth straight League Cup on a rainy Sunday afternoon. In a goalless stalemate, Rush and Kennedy had goals ruled out while Everton claimed a penalty after Hansen allegedly handled in the area (dark mutterings about Alan Hand-sen could be heard in the vicinity of Goodison Park for a very long time). The abiding image of the afternoon is of the two teams mingling at Wembley for a post-match photo, Alan Kennedy donning a blue beanie hat, John Bailey a red.

6. Everton replay, 1-0, 28 March 1984
The replay at Maine Road three days later was settled by Graeme Souness's magnificent swivel and strike on 21 minutes in front of 52,089 fans, one of whom attempted to give a non-plussed Souey a cuddle as he was presented with the Milk Cup. If you're reading this, sir, we salute you… and have you still got that jumper?

7. Arsenal 1-2, 5 April 1987
Liverpool never lose when Ian Rush scores… a record that lasted from 9 September 1981 until this day in 1987. Rush put the Reds in front in the first-half following great work by Craig Johnston and Steve McMahon, but Charlie Nicholas equalised just before the break in a goalmouth scramble and, seven minutes from time, substitute Perry Groves raced down the left wing to set up Charlie Nick for the winner.

8. Bolton Wanderers 2-1, 2 April 1995

It took a lot to get Sir Stanley Matthews purring, but Steve McManaman's dribbling did just that in this Coca-Cola Cup final. Many likened the Liverpool No.17 with the England legend as Matthews presented McManaman with his man of the match award. The mesmerising Macca repeatedly jinked through the Bolton defence, shooting through the legs of keeper Keith Branagan in the first-half, then doubling Liverpool's lead after the interval, weaving past defenders and sidefooting home to earn Roy Evans his first and only trophy as Liverpool manager.

9. Birmingham City 1-1, won 5-4 on penalties, 2001

Gerard Houllier's men travelled to Cardiff's Millennium Stadium for the first time to face Trevor Francis's Division One side in the Worthington Cup final. Robbie Fowler's stunning long-range lob over the head of Blues keeper Ian Bennett looked to have won it for Liverpool, until Stephane Henchoz conceded a penalty in the last minute, duly converted by Darren Purse. Extra time couldn't separate the teams, so the Reds entered their first penalty shoot-out in a domestic final. Sander Westerveld was the hero, saving from Andy Johnson and enabling Jamie Carragher to net the clincher.

10. Manchester United 2-0, 2 March 2003

The Millennium Stadium roof was shut as Gerrard and Owen netted the goals that provided the only highlights of an otherwise dismal season. Gerrard's shot on 39 minutes deflected off Beckham into the net, and Owen sealed matters four minutes from time, following a perfect ball from Hamann. Man of the match was Jerzy Dudek, some consolation after his disastrous error against United three months earlier.

11. Chelsea 2-3, 27 February 2005

Rafael Benitez had guided his team to a domestic cup final in his first season, but despite John-Arne Riise's spectacular first-minute volley, the Reds couldn't extend their lead. After hanging on grimly, they conceded an equaliser with 11 minutes to go, Steven Gerrard deflecting Paulo Ferreira's free kick into the net. Didier Drogba and Mateja Kezman extended Chelsea's lead in extra time, before Antonio Nuñez pulled one back almost immediately to set up a thrilling but ultimately futile finale. The lasting memory of the afternoon, however, remains the image of a framed portrait of Rafa being paraded, Ayatollah-style, through the streets of Cardiff.

LEAST SUCCESSFUL SEASONS

Liverpool. Eleventh in Division Two. Might seem a long time ago, but the Reds weren't always among the greatest in the land

1. 1903/04	Division One	17th	17 defeats
2. 1906/07	Division One	15th	18 defeats
3. 1908/09	Division One	16th	17 defeats
4. 1913/14	Division One	16th	17 defeats
5. 1932/33	Division One	14th	17 defeats
6. 1933/34	Division One	18th	18 defeats
7. 1935/36	Division One	19th	17 defeats
8. 1936/37	Division One	18th	19 defeats
9. 1952/53	Division One	17th	20 defeats
10 1953/54	Division One	22nd	23 defeats
11. 1954/55	Division Two	11th	16 defeats

LEGENDARY PRE-WORLD WAR 2 PLAYERS

Heroes and idols from between the wars

1. Tom Bromilow 1919-30
The bashful Bromilow joined the club after tentatively inquiring if there was any possibility of a trial. He proved himself immediately, shrugging off his slight physique with constructive football and intelligent distribution, playing 374 matches for the club. Bromilow later became a coach in Amsterdam.

2. Harry Chambers 1919-28
The man they called Smiler had bow legs and a ferocious shot that ensured he topped the Liverpool scoring charts five seasons in a row. Born in Northumberland, he won eight caps for England and finished his Liverpool career with 151 goals.

3. Dick Forshaw 1919-27
Lean and tall, Forshaw could play at centre-forward or inside-right, and struck up a useful partnership with Harry Chambers after joining the club from Middlesbrough. A consistent performer, Forshaw made 287 appearances and scored 124 goals for Liverpool before crossing Stanley Park to join Everton.

4. Gordon Hodgson 1925-36
Dixie Dean might have ruled the goalscoring roost on Merseyside in the 1930s, but

the South African ran him close with 240 goals in the red shirt. Hodgson's 36 strikes in the 1930/31 season established a club record. He even found time to play 50 matches for Lancashire CCC, and it was said he could hit a baseball like Babe Ruth.

5. Fred Hopkin 1921-31
Hopkin's first goal for the club in 1921 isn't likely to be forgotten, given that it was followed immediately by a fire in the main stand. The balding winger created countless chances for Liverpool's frontmen in a career encompassing ten seasons.

> HOPKIN'S FIRST GOAL ISN'T LIKELY TO BE FORGOTTEN – IT WAS FOLLOWED BY A FIRE IN THE MAIN STAND

6. James Jackson 1925-33
Nicknamed the Parson due to his ecclesiastical leanings, Jackson is believed to be the only Liverpool player to have become a minister after retirement. The defender skippered the team in 1928 and relished his ferocious derby battles with Dixie Dean. He studied Greek and philosophy at Cambridge University.

7. Jack Balmer 1935-52
Balmer's uncles had represented Everton before World War 1 and he was once on the books at Goodison. After arriving at Anfield in 1935, however, Balmer became a Liverpool hero thanks to his scoring prowess which once saw him score hat-tricks in three consecutive league matches.

8. Matt Busby 1935-40
The elegant Scot arrived in 1936 from Manchester City as an experienced right-half, schooled in the effective distribution of the ball. Busby captained the team and later took new signing Bob Paisley under his wing. He made 125 appearances for the Reds in a playing career cut short by World War 2.

9. Alf Hanson 1932-38
It was said of Hanson that he could put the fear of God into goalkeepers as he raided down the left wing and despatched pinpoint crosses. Born in Bootle, he was spotted playing for a local amateur team; he was appearing for the first team a year later. A ship's plumber by trade, he also represented England at baseball.

10. Berry Nieuwenhuys 1933-47
The South African proved a massive success on the left wing, providing pace, trickery and a thunderbolt shot. Nicknamed Nivvy, he made 260 appearances for the Reds, scoring 79 goals, and served in the RAF during World War 2.

11. Phil Taylor 1935-54

The man who preceded Bill Shankly as manager, Taylor served with distinction as a player for almost 20 years. He made 345 appearances as a centre-half blessed with an intelligent reading of the game and the knack of scoring crucial goals.

LIFE ACCORDING TO SHANKS

Football's most quoted – and misquoted – genius

1. "The socialism I believe in is everyone working for each other, everyone having a share of the rewards. It's the way I see football. It's the way I see life."

2. "It's great grass at Anfield. Professional grass."

3. "At a football club, there's a holy trinity – the players, the manager and the supporters. Directors don't come into it. They are only there to sign the cheques, not to make them out. We'll do that, they just sign them."

4. "I'm just one of the people who stands on the Kop. They think the same as I do, and I think the same as they do. It's a kind of marriage of people who like each other."

5. "Of course I didn't take my wife to see Rochdale as an anniversary present. It was her birthday. Would I have got married during the football season? Anyway, it was Rochdale reserves."

6. "If you can't make decisions in life, you're a bloody menace. You'd be better becoming an MP!"

7. "It's a 90-minute game for sure. I used to train for a 180-minute game so when the whistle blew at the end of the match I could have played another 90 minutes."

8. "If Everton were playing at the bottom of the garden, I'd draw the curtains."

9. "The trouble with referees is they know the rules, but they do not know the game."

10. "What a great day for football – all we need is some green grass and a ball."

11. "I was only in the game for the love of football. And I wanted to bring back happiness to the people of Liverpool."

LIGHTS, CAMERA, ACTION

11 classic moments from film and TV

1. The Ed Sullivan Show

It's May 1964 and as Merseybeat mania sweeps the USA, the Reds appear on the nation's most popular variety show during their tour of North America, singing *You'll Never Walk Alone* alongside fellow guests Gerry and the Pacemakers.

2. Find A Commentator

In 1969, the BBC attempted to unearth a new football commentator ahead of the Mexico World Cup, running a Eurovision-style competition featuring the likes of Ed Stewart, Tony Adamson and Ian St John, assessed on factors such as interpretation and presentation. St John reckoned he only came second to winner Idwal Robling because "that well-known Scots-hater Alf Ramsey" had the casting vote.

3. Kick-off

The immaculate timing of John Toshack and Kevin Keegan's strike partnership convinced some people that they must be psychic. In 1973, Granada Television put it to the test with a scientific experiment that saw K.K. and Tosh attempt to transmit colours and shapes on cards to each other using brainwaves. Tosh got 16 out of 24 right, but later admitted he'd seen the cards reflected in the camera lens.

4. Superstars

From the world of international sport, come… The Superstars! In 1976, Kevin Keegan participated in the gladiatorial sporting contest but came a cropper in the cycle race, crashing to the track and having half his skin ripped off in the process.

5. Escape To Victory

Prior to terrorising defences as a goalscoring midfielder for the Reds, John Wark starred alongside Michael Caine, Sylvester Stallone and Pelé in John Huston's dire 1981 PoW football movie taking on the plum role of Arthur Hayes.

6. Punchlines

For reasons that remain unclear, in 1983 Bruce Grobbelaar sparred with host Lennie Bennett on one edition of ITV's Saturday night quiz show *Punchlines*. History does not record if he went home having won a new toaster.

7. Boys From The Blackstuff

In 1982 Graeme Souness and Sammy Lee met Yosser Hughes in Alan Bleasdale's *Boys From The Blackstuff*. "You're Graeme Souness, aren't ya? You're famous. I'm

Yosser Hughes. You look like me. Magnum as well. A detective. He used to be on television. An American. I could have been a footballer. But I had a paper round."

8. Scully
Kenny Dalglish had a regular cameo role in the 1984 Channel 4 adaptation of Bleasdale's stories about Franny Scully, the Reds-obsessed teenage Scouse daydreamer played by Andrew Schofield. The opening titles featured Schofield running out before a Kop chanting "There's only one Franny Scully" (filmed before the 1983 derby at Anfield). Bruce Grobbelaar and Ian St John had cameo roles.

9. Bend It Like Beckham
In 2002 Alan Hansen made a brief cameo as himself alongside Gary Lineker and John Barnes, in the dreams of the wannabe footballer played by Parminder Nagra. By all accounts, Hansen and co needed multiple takes to get their lines right.

10. Merseybeat
Danny Murphy starred alongside his wife (then girlfriend) Joanna Taylor in the BBC police drama in 2004, playing himself making a presentation to a girls football team, and in a dramatic sub-plot, facing the prospect of getting nicked by the station's resident Everton supporter for driving with illegal tyres.

11. Hero To Zero
In 2000 Michael Owen had a regular cameo role in a children's BBC drama about troubled teenage footballer Charlie Brice, in which his poster of Owen magically came to life to offer him advice.

LIVERPOOL FC LANDMARKS

From the birthplace of the club to Shankly's front room...

1. The Sandon
Just a Jerzy Dudek goal kick from the Kop, this pub on Oakfield Road is where the Liverpool players used to get changed in the club's formative days.

2. 30 Bellefield Avenue
The West Derby home of Bill and Nessie Shankly for 22 years until his death, where he would invite in fans who knocked on the door for a chat and a cup of tea. It overlooked Everton's training ground and playing fields where Shankly would regularly join local youngsters for a kick-about.

3. St George's Hall

Home to many a homecoming for Liverpool's conquering heroes, most notably after the European Cup final of 1977, when Emlyn Hughes memorably attempted to whip up the crowd into a chorus of "Liverpool are magic, Everton are tragic".

4. The Falcon

Phil Thompson's local in Kirkby, where he triumphantly took the European Cup in a velvet bag after captaining the team to victory against Real Madrid in 1981.

5. Alsop School

The Walton comprehensive where Gerard Houllier taught in 1969. He became a Liverpool fan as he stood on the Kop for the 10-0 thrashing of Dundalk.

6. Glenbuck, Ayrshire

The Scottish mining village was the birthplace of Shankly and a plaque there now commemorates Shankly and the 55 pro-footballers the community produced.

7. Spion Kop, South Africa

The famous terrace at Anfield is named after a battle (in Natal) between Boer and British forces in January 1900. In Afrikaans *Spioenkop* means 'lookout hill'.

8. Holiday Inn

Now the Moat House hotel, the Holiday Inn on Paradise Street was the temporary home to many a new Liverpool arrival including Kenny Dalglish and Paul Walsh.

9. Cream

Roy Evans once banned Liverpool players from this "superclub" – founded by an Evertonian. Robbie Fowler, Jamie Redknapp and David James were all seen in there at one time or another, and it was where Steve McManaman met his future wife.

10. The Great Eastern

When Brunel's steamship was broken up at Rock Ferry in 1889, many of its fittings remained on Merseyside. Club officials, looking for a flagpole for Anfield, bought one of the masts and it was floated across the Mersey and hauled up to Anfield.

11. The Grafton

The infamous Liverpool nightspot on West Derby Road, as celebrated in the famous banner seen at Galatasaray in 2001: "Welcome to hell, my arse! If you think this is bad, try the Grafton on a Friday night!"

11. LAST CHAMPIONSHIP-WINNERS

Grobbelaar

Nicol Hysen Hansen (Gillespie) Burrows (Houghton)

Venison Molby McMahon Barnes

Rush Rosenthal

The team that clinched Liverpool's 18th and last championship, beating QPR 2-1 on 28 April 1990.

LOCAL HEROES

The Reds with a heart as big as Liverpool…

1. **John Aldridge** Garston
2. **Ian Callaghan** Toxteth
3. **Jamie Carragher** Bootle
4. **Robbie Fowler** Toxteth
5. **Steven Gerrard** Huyton
6. **Terry McDermott** Kirkby
7. **Steve McMahon** Huyton
8. **Steve McManaman** Kirkdale
9. **Ronnie Moran** Crosby
10. **Tommy Smith** Kirkdale
11. **Phil Thompson** Kirkby

MAJESTIC ROBBIE FOWLER MOMENTS

God's job's a good'un…

1. The appeal against the David Seaman penalty decision at Highbury in 1997.
2. The overhead flick and blast into the net against Brann Bergen in 1997.
3. The 'support the dockers' T-shirt displayed in the same match.
4. The dance across the box and shot into the bottom corner against Alaves in 2001.
5. The feint and clip over Peter Schmeichel at Anfield in December 1995.
6. The audacious overhead kick to clinch a Champions League spot at Charlton.
7. The belting long-range volley against Birmingham in the 2001 League Cup final.
8. The drilled finish – and dive into the net – in the first 4-3 against Newcastle in 1996.
9. The last-minute powered header to secure the second 4-3 against Newcastle.
10. The angled blast and cheeky chip at Old Trafford on Cantona's return in 1995.
11. The first-time shot that beat Villa's Bosnich off the post in the 1996 Cup semi.

MANAGEMENT MATERIAL

Some of the best bosses in the business learned their craft playing for Liverpool

1. John Aldridge
Aldo enjoyed five decent seasons at Tranmere Rovers, taking them to the League Cup final in 2000 (they lost to Leicester). Rovers also enjoyed good runs in the FA Cup, producing one of the greatest ever comebacks in 2001 to overhaul a three-goal half-time deficit against Southampton and run out 4-3 winners.

2. John Barnes
Reunited with director of football Kenny Dalglish at Celtic in 1999, but Digger's managerial career stalled after just 29 matches, not least thanks to a notorious cup upset at the hands of Inverness Caley Thistle.

3. Keith Burkinshaw
He played just one match for Liverpool, in 1955, but General Burkinshaw later assembled the attractive Tottenham team of Hoddle and Ardiles that won two FA Cups and the UEFA Cup in the early 1980s.

4. Matt Busby
He played at wing-half for Liverpool in the 1930s and turned down a coaching post at Anfield after World War 2 to take up the manager's job at Manchester United. Became the first manager of an English team to lift the European Cup.

5. Kevin Keegan
He'd have loved to have steered Newcastle to the title in 1996, but failed and six months later he was gone. Appointments at Fulham, England and Man City have produced familiar emotional patterns of exhilaration, frustration and resignation.

THE DRILLED FINISH, AND DIVE INTO THE NET, IN THE FIRST 4-3 AGAINST NEWCASTLE

6. Jimmy Melia
In 1983, the former Red inside-forward pulled on his dancing shoes and tripped the light fantastic all the way to Wembley with Brighton, but Gordon Smith's last-gasp miss prevented Jim's Seagulls from beating Manchester United to the Cup.

7. Gordon Milne
Following an early apprenticeship as player-manager at Wigan Athletic, the former midfielder became a top-flight boss at Coventry City between 1974 and 1981, and at Leicester City from 1982 to 1986. He spent seven years in charge at Besiktas in Turkey, and more recently has acted as director of football at Newcastle United.

8. Steve Nicol
One of the most respected coaches in the US, he guided New England Revolution to the brink of the 2002 MLS championship and just missed out on the 2003 play-off.

9. Karl-Heinz Riedle
Took temporary charge at Fulham for seven matches in the spring of 2000, assisted by his old Liverpool boss Roy Evans, but has yet to be tempted back into the dugout.

10. Graeme Souness
A frustrating period in the Liverpool dugout aside, Souey has enjoyed a successful career with Rangers, Galatasaray, Southampton, Torino, Benfica, Blackburn and Newcastle. Best forget Ali Dia and planting the Gala flag on Fenerbahce's centrespot.

11. John Toshack
Tosh experienced a meteoric induction taking Swansea City from Division Four to the top of the league, before stints at Sporting Lisbon, Real Sociedad (three times), Real Madrid (twice), Deportivo, Besiktas, St Etienne, Catania and now Wales.

MEMORABLE AWAY KITS
From white to yellow to silver to racing green to ecru and back again

1. The original 1960s onwards
In the glory days of the 1960s and 1970s, the away shirt wasn't a fashion statement to be worn down the pub, it was just something the team had to wear when we played at Highbury or Old Trafford. Hence the sheer simplicity of those white shirts with a round or v-neck collar and, of course, a Liver Bird on our chests.

2. Umbro/Yellow with red pinstripes 1982-85
Around the turn of the decade, it was decreed that white was out and yellow was in. Sported by Rushie and co from Teesside to Tokyo, 1982 also saw the subtle introduction of red pinstripes by Umbro, for that City trader's weekend-off image.

3. Adidas/White 1985-87
It's 1985 and Liverpool's strip is now the responsibility of Adidas. Once again the away shirt is white. With *Miami Vice* at its height, Don Johnson's white suits might have had a big influence. Possibly. Students of fashion might care to observe that it could be worn with black, red or white shorts. And they were short back then, too.

4. Adidas/Silver 1987-91
Back then, Liverpool were winning so much silver it was a natural progression that we should actually wear it. There were two incarnations, one with shiny stripes which bridged the sponsorship switch from Crown Paints to Candy, and one with a shiny, Pringle-style printed pattern introduced in 1989. Both effortlessly cool.

5. Adidas/Green 1991-93
Racing green with three thick white stripes across the shoulder. They even held test games at Anfield to ensure that the likes of Dean Saunders and Istvan Kozma could tell each other apart from the pitch. Which doesn't explain why we never won in the thing. Famously worn against Spartak Moscow in 1992, when they wore a red Adidas kit identical to Liverpool's home strip, confusing the hell out of everyone.

6. Adidas/Green and white 1993/94
"Green sleeves was my delight" – especially when Robbie Fowler and Steve McManaman ran rings around the likes of Swindon Town in this shortlived white number, with green arms and three thick Adidas stripes either side of the chest.

7. Adidas/Green and white quarters 1995/96
Perhaps the lesser of Liverpool's sartorial indiscretions on FA Cup final day 1996, this green-and-white quartered affair was infinitely more suited to rugby union. Indelibly linked with Robbie Fowler's bleached-blond period.

8. Adidas/Orange 1995/96
Briefly Liverpool's third strip, this distinctive, bright gold-and-black design was associated with the Razor Ruddock era. Orange is not the most flattering of colours and plastering the thing in Liver Birds did little to help.

9. Reebok/Ecru 1996/97
Beige is the new black, so they told us, and Liverpool attired themselves in a number technically called ecru, but actually looked a bit like if you'd washed your whites with your jeans. Launched at a photocall with Steve "John" McManaman, Rob "Paul" Jones, Jason "George" McAteer and Stan "Ringo" Collymore dressed up as The Beatles.

10. Reebok/Gold and navy 2000/01
This golden Reebok strip, with navy collar, trim and shorts, will always be linked with Houllier's Treble season – in particular with Michael Owen's double in the 2001 FA Cup final against Arsenal, not to mention his audacious strikes against Roma.

11. Reebok/Black 2002/03
Liverpool's black kit (with grey sleeves) was unpopular with fans and management alike, not least because the combination of colours made it difficult to pick players out. Its Premiership debut at Aston Villa proved particularly tricky.

MEMORABLE FA CUP TIES

It's still the biggest cup in football. Here's 11 classic Reds encounters

1. Manchester City 0-0, fifth round, 1956
One of the biggest footballing injustices in Liverpool's history. Billy Liddell looked to have fired the Reds into the last eight with a thunderous last-minute shot, only for the referee to chalk it off, claiming he'd blown for time while the ball was in mid-air.

2. Chelsea 2-0, semi-final, 1965
Three days after a draining European Cup play-off against Cologne, the Reds regrouped to face the Blues at Villa Park. They survived a disallowed strike by John Mortimore to take the lead through Peter Thompson, and when Chopper Harris hauled down the Saint in the box, Roger Hunt netted the penalty.

3. Leicester City 3-1, semi-final replay, 1974
The travelling Kop descends on the Holte End for this replay following a goalless draw at Old Trafford the previous Saturday. Toshack and Keegan in their pomp secure Liverpool's Wembley ticket, the second goal coming from a devastating volley from Keegan. Cue mass pitch invasion on the final whistle.

4. Grimsby Town 5-0, third round, 1979/80
Listed here solely due to the Kop enlivening a routine third-round romp against the Mariners by saluting their heroes in suitably aquatic style. Take a bow, Kenny Dogfish, Jimmy Plaice, Stingray Kennedy, Terry Mackerel…

5. Arsenal 0-0, 1-1, 1-1, 0-1, semi-final 1979/80
In the space of 18 days, Liverpool and Arsenal had to play their semi-final four times to settle the deadlock. The first match at Hillsborough ended goalless, the second 1-1, the third saw Alan Sunderland score after 13 seconds only for Dalglish to equalise on 90 minutes, and the decider at Highfield Road was settled by Brian Talbot. Five goals, seven hours of football, utter dejection… bring back marathon cup ties.

> IN THE SPACE OF 18 DAYS, LIVERPOOL AND ARSENAL PLAYED THEIR FA CUP SEMI-FINAL. FOUR TIMES

6. Newcastle United 4-0, third round, 1983/84
Billed as Kevin Keegan's final return to Anfield during his retirement season, the reunion all turned a bit sour for K.K. in this Friday night live match. Michael Robinson, Craig Johnston and Ian Rush with two put the Reds into the fourth round.

7. Manchester United 2-2, semi-final, 1984/85
The Goodison Park clock stands at 5.15, United are leading 2-1 and the Reds are almost dead and buried. Then Ian Rush heads towards goal, Gary Bailey parries it and the mighty Paul Walsh is on hand to bundle it over the line with his belly. The replay, however, is best forgotten.

8. Watford 2-1, sixth round replay, 1985/86
It's a freezing Monday night at Vicarage Road, John Barnes has put Watford in front

and there are just four minutes left. Rush is brought down in the box, big Jan converts the penalty and Rush himself makes it 2-1 in extra time.

9. Nottingham Forest 2-1, semi-final, 1987/88
Liverpool had lost only their second league match of the season to Forest seven days earlier, but it had no bearing on this semi. Digger defied the headlines claiming defender Steve Chettle was going to have "Barnes on toast" and inspired a win crowned by John Aldridge's memorable volleyed goal of the season.

10. Portsmouth 1-1, semi-final, 1991/92
Pompey are just ten minutes away from Wembley, having taken this semi at Highbury into extra time before Darren Anderton put them in front. But three minutes from time, a pearl of a free kick from John Barnes hits the post, Ronnie Whelan nets the rebound, and the Reds win the replay on penalties at the Villa.

11. Aston Villa 3-0, semi-final, 1995/96
Robbie Fowler emphatically booked Liverpool's place in the final with two goals at Old Trafford. The first is a glancing header at the Stretford End, the second a memorable dipping volley past Mark Bosnich that cracks satisfyingly off the post and into the net four minutes from the end. McAteer makes it three on 90 minutes.

MISSED PENALTIES
11 spot-kicks

1. **Ronnie Moran** v Swansea Town 1-2 (FA Cup 1964)
2. **Kevin Keegan/Tommy Smith** both v Tottenham Hotspur 1-1 (1973)
3. **Terry McDermott** v Ipswich Town 1-1 (1980)
4. **Phil Neal** v Brighton 1-2 (FA Cup 1983)
5. **John Wark** v Everton 0-1 (1985)
6. **Ian Rush** v Aston Villa 2-2 (1985)
7. **Jan Molby** v QPR 2-2 (Milk Cup 1986)
8. **John Aldridge** v Wimbledon 0-1 (FA Cup final 1988)
9. **John Barnes/Mike Marsh** both v QPR 1-0 (1993)
10. **Robbie Fowler** v Arsenal 2-1 (1997)
11. **Michael Owen** v Portsmouth 0-1 (FA Cup 2004)

MOST-CAPPED ENGLAND INTERNATIONALS

The Reds that roared for the Three Lions

1. **John Barnes** 79
2. **Michael Owen** 67
3. **Kevin Keegan** 63
4. **Emlyn Hughes** 62
5. **Ray Clemence** 61
6. **Peter Beardsley** 59
7. **Paul Ince** 53
8. **Phil Neal** 50
9. **Mark Wright** 45
10. **Emile Heskey** 43
11. **Phil Thompson** 42

MOST EXPENSIVE SALES

And the Reds who exited Anfield for a hefty price tag

1. **Robbie Fowler** £12.75m to Leeds United, 2001
2. **Michael Owen** £8m to Real Madrid, 2004
3. **Stan Collymore** £7.5m to Aston Villa, 1997
4. **Emile Heskey** £6.25m to Birmingham City, 2004
5. **Dominic Matteo** £4.75m to Leeds United, 2000
6. **Jason McAteer** £4m to Blackburn Rovers, 1999
   Christian Ziege £4m to Tottenham Hotspur, 2001
8. **Sander Westerveld** £4m to o Real Sociedad, 2001
   Nick Barmby £3.75m to Leed United, 2002
10. **Ian Rush** £3.2m to Juventus, 1986
11. **Stephen Wright** £3m to Sunderland, 2002

MOST EXPENSIVE SIGNINGS

The players on whom Liverpool splashed the cash, not all of whom were value

1. **Djibril Cisse** £14.5m from Auxerre, 2004
2. **Emile Heskey** £11m from Leicester City, 2000
3. **Xabi Alonso** £10.7m from Real Sociedad, 2004

4. El Hadji Diouf £10m from Lens, 2002
5. Stan Collymore £8.5m from Nottingham Forest, 1995
6. Dietmar Hamann £8m from Newcastle United, 1999
7. Fernando Morientes £6.3m from Real Madrid, 2005
8. Nick Barmby £6m from Everton, 2000
   Chris Kirkland £6m from Coventry City, 2001
   Luis Garcia £6m from Barcelona, 2004
11. Christian Ziege £5.5m from Middlesbrough, 2000

MUSICAL FANS

With the planet's finest musical heritage, it's no surprise there's so many musicians

1. John Power Cast
2. Elvis Costello
3. Dr Dre NWA
4. Pete Wylie Wah!
5. Melanie C Spice Girls
6. James Walsh Starsailor
7. Peter Hooton The Farm
8. Iain Broudie Lightning Seeds
9. Sean Moore Manic Street Preachers
10. Ian McCulloch Echo and the Bunnymen
11. Courtney Love Hole

NEW YEAR VICTORIES

11 days it was worth braving a hangover to see the Reds ring in the new

1. Blackpool 2 Liverpool 3 2 January 1965
Roger Hunt's double and a late strike from Ian St John secure the two points for
Shankly's team beside the seaside.

2. Liverpool 2 Manchester United 1 1 January 1966
Gordon Milne's late, late winner in the 88th minute sent the Kop into ecstasy, Tommy Smith having netted Liverpool's first.

3. Liverpool 2 Sunderland 0 1 January 1977
Ray Kennedy and Phil Thompson maintained Liverpool's pursuit for the Treble.

4. Liverpool 2 Middlesbrough 0 2 January 1978
The Reds follow up a New Year's Eve defeat by Newcastle by securing a north-east double, David Johnson and Steve Heighway netting the goals.

5. Swansea City 0 Liverpool 4 2 January 1982
The Reds dump Toshack's Swansea out of the FA Cup in Graeme Souness's first match as captain, Ian Rush grabbing two goals.

6. Liverpool 5 Notts County 1 1 January 1983
Ian Rush's hat-trick and a double from Kenny Dalglish destroy the Magpies, making Phil Neal's missed penalty irrelevant.

7. Liverpool 4 Coventry City 0 1 January 1988
The Reds score four for the eighth time of the 1987/88 season, with Peter Beardsley scoring twice, and John Aldridge and Ray Houghton adding the rest.

8. Liverpool 3 Leeds United 0 1 January 1991
John Barnes put Liverpool in front after just seven minutes, and Ronnie Rosenthal and Ian Rush also netted in a cruise for the Reds.

9. Ipswich Town 1 Liverpool 2 1 January 1994
Reds fans had Neil Ruddock and Ian Rush to thank for this win, Liverpool's first Premiership away success since August.

10. Liverpool 4 Norwich City 0 2 January 1995
Fowler notched up two after John Scales put Liverpool in front, Rush taking the fourth.

11. Liverpool 4 Nottingham Forest 2 1 January 1996
The Reds had to mount a fightback after going 2-1 down, Robbie Fowler grabbing two goals before Stan Collymore and a late Colin Cooper own goal sealed it.

NICKNAMES

So who was named after a character from One Flew Over The Cuckoo's Nest?

1. Rowdy Ron Yeats
After Rowdy Yates, Clint Eastwood's character in *Rawhide*.

2. The Flying Pig Tommy Lawrence
Due to his ability to make athletic saves despite a less than aerodynamic physique.

3. Big Bamber and Little Bamber Steve Heighway and Brian Hall
Both had degrees, hence candidates for Bamber Gascoigne's *University Challenge*.

4. Andy McDaft Kevin Keegan
Due to K.K.'s frequent bouts of madcap behaviour.

5. Barney Rubble Alan Kennedy
Looked a bit like Fred Flintstone's prehistoric sidekick.

6. Cheswick Terry McDermott
After the character from the classic asylum comedy *One Flew Over The Cuckoo's Nest*.

7. Rambo Jan Molby
Played like Cruyff, looked like Stallone…

8. Chopsy Steve Nicol
Because of the way he pronounced chips. Also known as Chico.

9. Digger John Barnes
Named after Digger Barnes from *Dallas*.

10. God Robbie Fowler
No explanation needed.

11. Basil Dietmar Hamann
An alleged resemblance to John Cleese… and that Germans episode of *Fawlty Towers*.

> JAN MOLBY WAS NICKNAMED RAMBO, THANKS TO A STRIKING RESEMBLANCE TO SLY STALLONE

OBSCURE EUROPEAN DESTINATIONS

"We're all going to Esch-Sur-Alzette…"

1. **Vladikavkaz, Russia** Alania Vladikavkaz, 1995
2. **Oulu, Finland** OPS, 1980
3. **Ploiseti, Romania** Petrolul Ploiesti, 1967
4. **Esch-Sur-Alzette, Luxembourg** Jeunesse Esch, 1973
5. **Dramman, Norway** Stromsgodset, 1974
6. **Valkeakoski, Finland** FC Haka, 2001
7. **Trabzon, Turkey** Trabzonspor, 1976
8. **Kosice, Slovakia** FC Kosice, 1998
9. **Anjalankoski, Finland** MyPa 47, 1996
10. **Wroclaw, Poland** Slask Wroclaw, 1975
11. **Ljubljana, Slovenia** Olimpija Ljubljana, 2003

OLDEST LEAGUE PLAYERS

It's experience that counts, as these 11 time-honoured masters of the game prove

1. **Ted Doig** 41 years, 165 days
2. **Ephraim Longworth** 40 years, 202 days
3. **Elisha Scott** 39 years, 181 days
4. **Kenny Dalglish** 39 years, 58 days
5. **Billy Liddell** 38 years, 234 days
6. **Billy Dunlop** 37 years, 277 days
7. **Gary McAllister** 37 years, 137 days
8. **Don McKinley** 37 years, 38 days
9. **Tom Lucas** 37 years, 32 days
10. **Paul Jones** 36 years, 267 days
11. **Bruce Grobbelaar** 36 years, 136 days

ONE-GAME WONDERS

Just to play one game for the Reds would be a dream. This lot made it a reality

1. **Tom Lowry** v Wolves, 1965
2. **John Sealey** v Wolves, 1965
3. **David Wilson** v Blackpool, 1967
4. **Steve Arnold** v Manchester City, 1971
5. **Derek Brownbill** v Birmingham City, 1973
6. **Dave Rylands** v Doncaster Rovers, 1974
7. **Kevin Kewley** v Middlesbrough, 1978
8. **Colin Russell** v Sunderland, 1981
9. **Brian Mooney** v Fulham, 1986
10. **Barry Jones** v Kuusysi Lahti, 1991
11. **Leyton Maxwell** v Hull City, 1999

ONE-GOAL WONDERS

They never scored again for the Reds but still scored more than Stephane Henchoz

1. **Bobby Campbell** v Bristol Rovers, 1960
2. **Phil Ferns** v Blackburn Rovers, 1964
3. **John Sealey** v Wolves, 1965
4. **Alan Waddle** v Everton, 1973
5. **Avi Cohen** v Aston Villa, 1980
6. **Howard Gayle** v Tottenham Hotspur, 1981
7. **Gary Ablett** v Nottingham Forest, 1987
8. **Nick Tanner** v Everton, 1991
9. **Phil Babb** v Coventry City, 1996
10. **Leyton Maxwell** v Hull City, 1999
11. **Stephen Wright** v Borussia Dortmund, 2001

LIVERPOOL HAVE
PLAYED EVERYWHERE,
FROM OULU, FINLAND
TO WROCLAW, POLAND

ORIGINAL PREMIERSHIP SQUAD NUMBERS FROM 1993/94

From one to 11, Liverpool's inaugural set of squad numbers

1. **Bruce Grobbelaar**
2. **Rob Jones**
3. **David Burrows**
4. **Steve Nicol**
5. **Mark Wright**
6. **Don Hutchison**
7. **Nigel Clough**
8. **Paul Stewart**
9. **Ian Rush**
10. **John Barnes**
11. **Mark Walters**

PEEL 'ON POOL

11 classic quotes from the late and legendary DJ

1. "I am still, at 59, a man who likes to fantasise. Mostly, I fantasise about being, as Jimmy Tarbuck apparently is, mates with the entire Liverpool squad."

2. "Kenny Dalglish once came into Radio 1 to record a programme, and I was going to take the kids in for a laying-on of hands."

3. "Football looms pretty large in our house – the wait for kitchen units in the right shade of red lasted over 18 months."

4. "At the first boarding school I went to, there were about 80 boys. Seventy-eight of them supported United, I supported Liverpool and there was one boy who wasn't interested in football. So my prejudice against United has been lifelong."

5. "As far as I'm concerned, the name of Alan Kennedy will echo down the centuries."

6. "I've never been one for autographs. I asked Sam Lightnin' Hopkins for his, Hendrix for his and I collected Billy Liddell's on a flyer for the Reynolds News before a match at Anfield in the 1950s."

7. "I have every right to be nostalgic about the stadium because two of my children have got the word 'Anfield' in their names. We might have to change their names if the club moves."

8. "My favourite season was the one when Liverpool were about 12th at Christmas, but then they started to climb. It was really romantic, like the Long March or something."

9. "The 1984 European Cup final was so tense. I was lying on the studio floor, and I'm not exactly sure what hyperventilating is, but I think I was doing it, so Kid Jensen had to do the first 20 minutes of my show."

10. "In a funny way I think Liverpool have swapped roles with Manchester United. In the 1980s, United were capable of being amazing and also capable of being unspeakably feeble, and I think there's still an element of that at Liverpool now."

11. "Next on Top Of The Pops, at number 18, it's Jennifer Rush, scoring more often than Ian Rush at the moment."

PENALTY KINGS

The men who were deadly from 12 yards out… most of the time, anyway

1. Jan Molby 41
2. Phil Neal 38
3. Billy Liddell 32
4. Tommy Smith 21
5. John Aldridge 17
   Terry McDermott 17
   Robbie Fowler 17
8. Gordon Hodgson 15
9. Michael Owen 13
10. Kevin Keegan 11
    Ronnie Moran 11

PERFORMING YOU'LL NEVER WALK ALONE

11 artists who have recorded the definitive Anfield anthem, take it away...

1. Gerry and the Pacemakers
2. Elvis Presley
3. Aretha Franklin
4. Johnny Cash
5. Frank Sinatra
6. José Carreras, Placido Domingo and Luciano Pavarotti
7. Barbra Streisand
8. Ray Charles
9. Shirley Bassey
10. Louis Armstrong
11. Olivia Newton-John

PLAYERS TURNED PUNDITS

They played a great game for Liverpool, now they talk one

1. Alan Hansen
The BBC's premier pundit since 1991. Hansen oozes the authority he brought to the Reds' defence on the *MOTD* desk. Can shut Peter Schmeichel up, too. Unbelievable.

2. Graeme Souness
Now spends Wednesday nights perched next to Richard Keys on a chrome stool, providing "been there, done that" insights to Sky's Champions League coverage.

3. Jim Beglin
Dry, incisive commentator's sidekick on ITV's coverage of the Champions League and also for Radio 5 Live.

4. Phil Thompson
Recently rejoined Sky's *Soccer Saturday* after five years as Gerard Houllier's deputy. Now scrutinising Liverpool's progress via monitor and headphones.

5. John Barnes
Digger has turned from punditry to presentation in recent seasons, leaving the ITV panel to strike out as Five's chief sporting anchorman.

6. Ray Houghton

Regularly appears on Irish television network RTE, as well as occasionally summarising for Five and presenting talkSPORT's *Golf Show*.

7. Nigel Spackman

Spackers is another regular alongside Jeff Stelling and company on Sky's *Soccer Saturday* results and instant punditry service.

8. Jamie Redknapp

The former midfield maestro has been successfully attempting to carve out a new career as a summariser for BBC television and radio.

9. John Aldridge

Now a passionate Liverpool summariser every Saturday afternoon for Radio City.

10. Alan Kennedy

Dispenses wit and wisdom on Century 105.4's nightly football phone-in.

11. Michael Robinson

Now one of the most famous faces in Spain, thanks to his role as producer and presenter of *El Dia Despues* on Canal Plus, a blend of action and humour.

PLAYERS WHO APPEARED IN EVERY LEAGUE GAME IN A SEASON

The ever-presents who never missed a match

1. Ray Clemence 1971/72, 1973/74, 1974/75, 1976/77, 1978/79
2. Phil Neal 1975/76, 1976/77, 1977/78, 1978/79, 1979/80, 1980/81, 1981/82, 1982/83, 1984/85
3. Kenny Dalglish 1977/78, 1978/79, 1979/80, 1981/82, 1982/83
4. Alan Kennedy 1982/83, 1983/84
5. Bruce Grobbelaar 1981/82, 1982/83, 1983/84, 1984/85, 1985/86, 1989/90
6. Steve Nicol 1987/88, 1988/89
7. Steve McMahon 1987/88, 1989/90
8. Ian Rush 1986/87, 1993/94
9. Robbie Fowler 1994/95, 1995/96
10. David James 1994/95, 1995/96, 1996/97
11. Sami Hyypia 1999/2000, 2003/04

PLAYERS WHO APPEARED IN THE EUROPEAN CHAMPIONSHIP

From Italy 80 to Portugal 04, the men who carried the flags across the continent

1. **Ray Clemence** England, 1980
2. **Terry McDermott** England, 1980
3. **John Barnes** England, 1988
4. **Ray Houghton** Republic of Ireland, 1988
5. **Steve McManaman** England, 1996
6. **Jamie Redknapp** England, 1996
7. **Vegard Heggem** Norway, 2000
8. **Vladimir Smicer** Czech Republic, 2000, 2004
9. **Sander Westerveld** Holland, 2000
10. **Milan Baros** Czech Republic, 2004
11. **Stephane Henchoz** Switzerland, 2004

PLAYERS WHO APPEARED IN THE WORLD CUP FINALS

11 Reds to have played on the biggest stage of all

1. **Laurie Hughes** England, 1950
2. **Alan A'Court** England, 1954
3. **Roger Hunt** England, 1966
4. **Kenny Dalglish** Scotland, 1978, 1982
5. **Phil Thompson** England, 1982
6. **Jan Molby** Denmark, 1986
7. **Peter Beardsley** England, 1990
8. **Steve Staunton** Republic of Ireland, 1990
9. **Stig Inge Bjornbye** Norway, 1994
10. **Michael Owen** England, 1998, 2002
11. **Dietmar Hamann** Germany, 2002

PLAYERS WHO SCORED OWN GOALS FOR LIVERPOOL

Some of football's biggest names have scored for the Reds...unintentionally

1. **Danny Blanchflower** Aston Villa, 1953
2. **Gary Sprake** Leeds United, 1967
3. **Sandy Brown** Everton, 1969

4. Dave Mackay Derby County, 1971
5. Tommy Wright Everton, 1972
6. John Bailey Everton, 1981
7. Steve Bruce Norwich City, 1984 and Manchester United, 1995
8. Paul McGrath Manchester United, 1985
9. Gordon Strachan Leeds United, 1992
10. Rio Ferdinand Leeds United, 2002
11. Titus Bramble Newcastle United, 2004

PLAYERS WITH MOST INTERNATIONAL CAPS

11 multi-capped Reds (not all won while at Liverpool)

1. Kenny Dalglish 102, Scotland
   Steve Staunton 102, Republic of Ireland
3. Jari Litmanen 93, Finland
4. Oyvind Leonhardsen 86, Norway
5. Brad Friedel 82, USA
6. John Barnes 79, England
7. Stig-Inge Bjornebye 75, Norway
   Dean Saunders 75, Wales
9. Ray Houghton 73, Republic of Ireland
   Ian Rush 73, Wales
11. Joey Jones 72, Wales

PREMIERSHIP PLAYERS WHO CHANGED SHIRT NUMBERS

11 Reds who played the numbers game

1. Robbie Fowler 23 to 9
2. Steven Gerrard 28 to 17 to 8
3. Michael Owen 18 to 9
4. Steve McManaman 17 to 7
5. Sami Hyypia 12 to 4
6. Vladimir Smicer 7 to 11
7. David James 13 to 1
8. Chris Kirkland 22 to 12
9. Paul Stewart 8 to 4
10. Jamie Redknapp 15 to 11
11. Steve Harkness 22 to 12

QUOTES ABOUT THE LIVERPOOL WAY

Get it, give it and move. The Anfield philosophy in their own words

1. "Just play. That's all they said. Nothing was pre-planned. The quality of the pass, the movement off the ball, everything came in training. The players were all intelligent, they knew when to go, when to stay. And never one of them put themselves before the team." *Kenny Dalglish*

2. "I was with the best club in the world. We knew at the start of each season when we were photographed with the trophies there was a fair chance they were going to be in the same picture the following year." *Graeme Souness*

3. "Time and again it was drummed into us. Football is a simple game – why complicate it?" *Sammy Lee*

4. "I'd kick my own brother if necessary… it's what being a professional footballer is all about." *Steve McMahon*

5. "People would say I was lazy, which I was, but I could read where the ball was going, so what was the point of running for it? I wasn't the best or the fastest, but I could read a good game." *Ray Kennedy*

6. "The players Bob Paisley bought were winners. We all wanted to win. It was simple – get it, give it and move. That's what was drummed into us. Don't stand and admire." *Terry McDermott*

7. "It was a privilege to be at Liverpool. It wasn't about money in those days. We'd have played for nothing." *Peter Cormack*

8. "When you had the artillery we had, you always felt comfortable going out to play. It was built into the team you'd have three players to pass to, within two seconds on the ball." *Jimmy Case*

9. "Liverpool are the most uncomplicated side in the world. They all drive forward when they've got the ball and they all get behind it when they haven't." *Joe Mercer*

10. "One season we used 14 players, an unbelievable feat. Squad rotation is one thing I wouldn't like now. Playing every week you develop an understanding." *Ian Callaghan*

11. "Liverpool was everything I wanted. A massive club, success and fantastic support. But whatever happened, it was fish and chips on the way home. I loved it." *Paul Walsh*

RAFA: HE CAME FROM SUNNY SPAIN TO HELP US WIN AGAIN

11 amazing facts about Rafael Benitez

1. Ten years ago he was working part-time at a Madrid sports centre, running its amateur football team.

2. He sharpened his football tactical awareness by staying up all night to learn the rules of strategy board game Stratego.

3. In the 1990s he spent a year studying football coaching methods in different countries, including spells at Manchester United and Arsenal.

4. His wife Montse has said Benitez shouts instructions to players during his sleep.

5. Benitez has a degree in physical education and once coached soccer players at Davis University in the USA.

6. He had a spell with Real Madrid as a player but never appeared for the first team.

7. In 1995 he was appointed coach of Real Valladolid but was sacked after 23 games.

8. In his first season in charge at Valencia, he led the club to their first La Liga championship in 31 years.

9. His Valencia team beat Liverpool twice in the Champions League in 2002/03 – 2-0 at the Mestalla and 1-0 at Anfield.

10. He fell out with his bosses at Valencia when he asked for the finance to buy a striker and was bought a winger instead, fuming, "I asked for a sofa and they bought me a standard lamp."

11. Benitez once banned his Valencia players from eating paella on Sundays.

RECORDS FEATURING LIVERPOOL TEAMS AND PLAYERS

It's not just The Anfield Rap...

1. Liverpool, Liverpool 1972
"There's something about the air in Liverpool!" The team recorded this in the early 1970s, featuring such lines as "so raise your hats and say hip-hip-hip-hooray!"

2. The Kop Choir LP 1972
They sang until they dropped on this classic recording of the Spion Kop in full throat on the Hallmark label. Now much sought after and can fetch up to £20.

3. We Can Do It 1977
Belted out by Ray Clemence in the Olympic Stadium team bath after the Reds had lifted the European Cup in Rome, this remake of The Rubettes hit climbed to No.15.

4. Hail To The Kop 1978
"Hail to the Kop! You know we love you, a lot." They don't write them like this European Cup final scarf-waver any more.

5. Head Over Heels In Love Kevin Keegan, 1979
Mighty Mouse had left Merseyside for Hamburg by the time he recorded this soaring ballad, which reached No. 31. Kev was made-up to hear it nominated Smash Of The Week by one DJ… but less delighted to hear it then smashed on air.

6. Side By Side Ray Clemence and Peter Shilton, 1980
The indomitable Clem was duelling with Shilts for the England jersey when they teamed up to record this arm-in-arm refrain, which failed to trouble the hit parade.

7. Liverpool (We're Never Gonna Stop) 1983
Featuring Alan Parry commentary samples, this cod-reggae effort could only reach
No. 54 as Paisley's men swept to their 14th championship.

8. Sitting On Top Of The World 1986
Kenny's Double side didn't get a lot wrong in 1986, but this disastrous singalong
was a rare exception, scraping to No. 50 in the charts.

9. The Pride Of Merseyside Joe Fagin, 1987
Not our former gaffer, but the fella who did the theme from *Auf Wiedersehen, Pet*.
Adapted by Craig Johnston from the Kop classic *With A Liverbird On My Chest*.

10. The Anfield Rap 1988
Johnston then devised the lyrics to the team's Cup final record, featuring the
seminal line "I come from Jamaica, my name is John Barnes, when I do my thing
the crowd goes bananas" and samples of Bill Shankly and Brian Moore.

11. Pass & Move Liverpool FC and The Bootroom Boyz, 1996
Described by John Peel as "possibly the best single of all time", this FA Cup tribute
featured Barnesy rapping and lyrics like "Sharp like Armani, Jamo is the saviour".

RED FOR BLUE, BLUE FOR RED

They crossed the Park to play for both Merseyside clubs

1. Andrew Hannah
The first man to captain both clubs, Hannah was a powerful defender for Everton
in the early 1890s before arriving at Anfield in 1893. He skippered his new club to
promotion during his first season, in which Liverpool didn't lose a league game.

2. Dick Forshaw
The potent inside-forward made 287 appearances for Liverpool in the 1920s before
he crossed Stanley Park in 1927. He is still the only player to have won league
championship medals for both sides.

3. Dave Hickson
The Cannonball Kid caused uproar in 1959 when he left the Blues to join Liverpool,
prompting fans to tear up their season tickets and one Reds supporter to run onto
the pitch during the striker's first match and give him a kiss.

4. David Johnson
The striker scored a derby winner as a 20-year-old against the Reds at Goodison in 1971, and after a stint at Ipswich Town he joined Liverpool in 1976, clinching a derby victory for the Reds in 1980. He rejoined Everton in 1982.

5. Steve McMahon
The boyhood Everton ballboy is the second player to have captained both clubs. The fearless midfielder left Everton in 1983, turning down Liverpool's offer and joining Aston Villa instead. He finally signed for the Reds in 1985, scoring against Everton in only his second appearance.

6. Kevin Sheedy
He of the "trusty left foot" never quite broke through at Anfield, making five first-team appearances before departing for Goodison Park, where his undoubted skill established him as a key member of Everton's successful teams of the 1980s.

7. David Burrows
Bugsy became a bit of a hit with the Liverpool fans, but by 1993 he had fallen out of favour with Graeme Souness and was sold to West Ham. In 1994, he returned to Merseyside to join Everton for a six-month spell.

8. Don Hutchison
The energetic midfielder made 59 appearances for Liverpool in the 1990s before joining West Ham and then Sheffield United, from whom he signed for Everton in 1998, making 79 appearances.

9. Peter Beardsley
The darling of the Kop was rashly sold by Graeme Souness to the Blues in 1991, and returned to haunt his former manager by scoring a late winner against Liverpool in the derby at Goodison Park in 1992. He had previously netted six against the Blues.

10. Nick Barmby
In 2000, the England midfielder became the first player since Hickson to leave Everton directly for Liverpool, and promptly repaid his £6m transfer fee with the opening goal in a 3-1 derby win. "He's red, he's white, he scored against the…"

11. Abel Xavier
The unmistakable Portuguese defender crossed Stanley Park to join Liverpool in 2002 for a fee of £800,000, becoming the 12th player to have appeared for both sides in a Merseyside derby.

REDS WHO PLAYED IN THE NORTH AMERICAN SOCCER LEAGUE

In the 1970s and 1980s, plenty of British stars headed for the land of cheerleaders

1. **Peter Beardsley** Vancouver Whitecaps, 1981-83
2. **Ian Callaghan** Fort Lauderdale Strikers, 1978
3. **Peter Cormack** Toronto City, 1967
4. **Roy Evans** Philadelphia Atoms, 1973
5. **David Fairclough** Toronto Blizzard, 1982
6. **Bruce Grobbelaar** Vancouver Whitecaps, 1979-80
7. **Steve Heighway** Minnesota Kicks, 1981
8. **Chris Lawler** Miami Toros, 1976
9. **Alec Lindsay** Oakland Stompers, 1978 and Toronto Blizzard, 1979
10. **Tommy Smith** Tampa Bay Rowdies, 1976 and Los Angeles Aztecs, 1978
11. **Graeme Souness** Montreal Olympic, 1972

RENOWNED POST-WAR PLAYERS

From the end of World War 2 to the arrival of Bill Shankly

1. Billy Liddell
It says everything about Liddell that the club was almost renamed Liddellpool in the forward's honour. The Scot was revered for his pace, power and dashing style and, moreover, his grace and humility, staying loyal to the club throughout their exile in Division Two. Perhaps the greatest man to ever pull on the red shirt.

2. Albert Stubbins
Even in his 80s, the Geordie would be greeted on his returns to Merseyside by admirers demanding to know if he'd brought his boots. The prolific centre-forward joined the Reds from Newcastle in a deal he learned about in a cinema, after a message was flashed on screen instructing him to report to St James' Park. Stubbins netted 83 goals in seven seasons at Anfield.

3. Alan A'Court
He might have sounded like one of Robin Hood's merry men, but the left-winger actually hailed from Rainhill. He possessed sublime control, speed and deadly crossing ability, making 382 appearances, the last of which came in Liverpool's first-ever European match against Reykjavik in 1964.

4. Laurie Hughes
The powerful, perceptive defender joined Liverpool straight after World War 2 and promptly helped the Reds to lift the championship. He played 326 matches in a long career at Anfield, making three appearances for England at the 1950 World Cup.

5. Bob Paisley
His incredible managerial record overshadows an impressive playing career for Liverpool as a tireless left-back noted for his remarkable long throw. Perhaps his greatest moment came when he scored the winning goal in the 1950 FA Cup semi-final against Everton, but tragically he was dropped for the final.

6. Bill Jones
The grandfather of Rob Jones, Bill was an adaptable and reliable footballer, who once played in five different positions in one season. In 1953 he scored the goals that kept Liverpool in Division One, and he could have also made the grade as a first-class cricketer. Jones was awarded the Military Medal in World War 2.

7. Eddie Spicer
Spicer's career ended in sadness, twice breaking his leg in rapid succession, but he served Liverpool with distinction as a defender tenacious in the tackle and reluctant to admit defeat. He made 168 appearances for the Reds, having also been decorated for bravery while serving with the Royal Marines.

8. Ray Lambert
Lambert joined Liverpool in 1936 at the record-breaking age of 13-and-a-half, but had to wait until the end of World War 2 for his breakthrough. He was a dedicated defender who started at centre-half but later moved to full-back, displaying coolness and keen positional sense over 11 seasons.

9. Dick White
A dependable presence in the Liverpool defence, replacing Laurie Hughes in 1955 after joining from Scunthorpe United. Fierce in the challenge, Dick was an astute distributor of the ball. He made 216 appearances for the Reds, scoring one goal.

10. Jimmy Payne
Payne joined Liverpool from local football in 1948. He had the talent that saw him compared with Matthews or Finney, but sadly he lacked the confidence to match. Despite some mesmerising dribbling skills and control, he never blossomed as he should have done, although 43 goals in 243 games is still an impressive record.

11. Willie Fagan
No relation to Joe, the red-haired Scot became renowned for his effective tactic of switching from inside-forward to centre-forward during the course of a match, invariably nicking a goal or two. He joined Liverpool in 1937 from Preston, where he played alongside Bill Shankly, and stayed at Anfield for 15 years.

ROWS, FEUDS AND GRUDGES

Those we have loathed, the back-page controversies and the simmering quarrels

1. Malcolm MacDonald
Supermac earned the everlasting enmity of Liverpool in the run-up to the 1974 FA Cup final. "I've scored in every round so far and I'm going to get one when we win at Wembley," declared the Newcastle No. 9. "Say your prayers, Reds!" Supermouth was silenced by Phil Thompson in a satisfying 3-0 exhibition.

2. Tony Wilson
The music impresario, broadcaster and professional Mancunian wound-up Reds prior to the 1978 European Cup final by donning a huge Bruges rosette on *Granada Report*.

3. Gerald Sinstadt
Two days after the Reds had been knocked out of the European Cup by Nottingham Forest, the Granada commentator infuriated Reds supporters by announcing: "The party's over, Liverpool!" and cueing in a montage of footage from the match to the song of the same name. On future assignments to Liverpool games, Sinstadt was serenaded by a chorus of "How's the party going now?"

4. Luton Town
The winter of 1987 brought a furious row over thousands of unsold sausage rolls. Luton were due to play an FA Cup replay at Anfield where the pitch was immaculate, but Luton claimed they couldn't reach Merseyside due to snow, incensing Liverpool, who distributed the excess pies to some no-doubt grateful local pensioners.

5. Dalglish v Ferguson
Following a prickly 3-3 draw on Easter Monday 1988, Ferguson loudly criticised the referee, announcing to the assembled media, "You need a miracle to win here." The passing Dalglish, cradling his baby, retorted, "You might as well talk to my baby daughter. You'll get more sense out of her."

6. Sandra Beardsley v Marina Dalglish

It was one of the footballing urban myths of the 1990s, that after Kenny Dalglish dropped his neighbour Peter Beardsley, their respective spouses did verbal battle over their Southport garden fence. Laughable, said Beardsley in his autobiography.

7. Grobbelaar v McManaman

It's the Merseyside derby of September 1993 and Steve McManaman hits a weak clearance that gifts Everton the lead at Goodison Park. Brucie castigates Shaggy, who starts yelling back at the keeper, who in turn tries to wring McManaman's neck.

8. Don Hutchison

The talented midfielder is forever remembered for an incident during a holiday to Ayia Napa involving a distinct lack of trousers, a strategically-placed Budweiser label and a holidaymaker's camera. Hutchison was fined £5,000, dropped, transfer-listed and shipped out to West Ham United.

9. Fowler v Ruddock

During a UEFA Cup trip to Spartak Vladikavkaz, Robbie Fowler and Neil Ruddock engaged in a dispute over Razor's shoes, which resulted in Fowler cutting up his £300 Gucci footwear and receiving a punch on the nose in a crowded airport lounge for his handiwork.

10. Robbie Fowler

In April 1999, Fowler responds to taunts about his recreational habits from Everton fans by celebrating a goal in the derby by getting down on his knees and pretending to sniff the goal line. Memorably, Gerard Houllier attempted to justify it by suggesting Fowler was merely pretending to be a cow eating grass.

11. DJ George v Roma

It's difficult to imagine that a major diplomatic incident could almost be sparked by a quick spin of *Arrivederci Roma*, but that happened in 2001 when Anfield announcer George Sephton rounded off a stormy match against AS Roma by playing the record, promptly enraging 2,000 visiting fans.

SCANDINAVIAN REDS

They came from the icy wastes of the north to be feted by Kopites

1. **Stig Inge Bjornbye** Elverum, Norway
2. **Vegard Heggem** Trondheim, Norway
3. **Glen Hysen** Gothenburg, Sweden
4. **Sami Hyypia** Porvoo, Finland
5. **Frode Kippe** Oslo, Norway
6. **Bjorn Tore Kvarme** Trondheim, Norway
7. **Oyvind Leonhardsen** Kristiansund, Norway
8. **Jari Litmanen** Lahti, Finland
9. **Jan Molby** Kolding, Denmark
10. **Torben Piechnik** Copenhagen, Denmark
11. **John Arne Riise** Aalesund, Norway

SCOTTISH REDS

A classic team of Macs

1. **Matt Busby** Orbiston, Lanarkshire
2. **Kenny Dalglish** Glasgow
3. **Alan Hansen** Sauchie, Clackmannanshire
4. **Billy Liddell** Dunfermline
5. **Tommy Lawrence** Dailly, Ayrshire
6. **Gary McAllister** Motherwell
7. **Steve Nicol** Irvine, Ayrshire
8. **Alex Raisbeck** Polmont, Stirlingshire
9. **Graeme Souness** Edinburgh
10. **Ian St John** Motherwell
11. **Ron Yeats** Aberdeen

SENDINGS OFF

Those memorable moments when Reds saw red

1. Ian St John v Coventry City 1967
The Saint turned sinner in a Boxing Day spat with Brian Lewis, although a Shankly ploy involving a boot-polish fake bruise in his nether regions got him off suspension.

2. Tommy Smith v Manchester City 1973
Despite Smithy's reputation, he was only sent off once in his career, when he told referee Clive Thomas to "sod off", as he euphemistically put it.

3. Kevin Keegan v Leeds United 1974
Not much charity in the first Charity Shield at Wembley as Keegan traded punches with Billy Bremner, resulting in red cards all round and shirts flung to the ground.

4. Terry McDermott v Everton 1979
McDermott headed for a premature appointment with the Radox after scrapping with Gary Stanley in a fiery encounter to earn the first sendings-off in derby history.

5. Mark Lawrenson v CSKA Sofia 1982
Lawro picked up Liverpool's first sending-off in two decades of continental competition for retaliation as the Reds crashed out of the European Cup.

6. Paul Walsh v Southampton 1987
The diminutive striker satisfyingly floored Southampton's giant Kevin Bond with a classic right-hook after the centre-half had spat at him during a Littlewoods Cup tie.

7. Bruce Grobbelaar v Spartak Moscow 1992
The Reds keeper earned a red card for bringing down Dmitri Radchenko in the box in this Cup Winners' Cup tie, resulting in Bugsy Burrows having to don the gloves.

8. Robbie Fowler v Everton 1997
God received his marching orders at Goodison Park in April 1997 after clashing with defender David Unsworth.

9. Sander Westerveld v Everton 1999
The Dutch keeper trudged to the Goodison dressing room after a bout of designer handbags with Franny Jeffers. Steve Staunton went in goal and played a blinder.

10. Michael Owen v Manchester United 1998

It wasn't a Good Friday for Owen as he received a second yellow card at Old Trafford for clattering into Ronny Johnsen, but the Reds hung on for a 1-1 draw.

11. Sami Hyypia v Manchester United 2003

The Finn received the red card after just three minutes at Old Trafford, in possibly Liverpool's fastest sending-off, for felling Ruud van Nistelrooy in the box.

SHOOTING DOWN THE GUNNERS

11 memorable performances against Arsenal

1. Liverpool 3 Arsenal 2 22 August 1964

"We're here in Beatleville," announced Kenneth Wolstenholme at the start of the first-ever *Match Of The Day*. Roger Hunt scored the first goal seen on the show, and two goals from fleetingly successful forward Gordon Wallace confirmed victory.

2. Arsenal 0 Liverpool 0 8 May 1972

On an extraordinary night at the down-to-the-wire climax of the championship, the Reds lose out to Derby County in a three-way battle for the title. If the referee hadn't ruled out John Toshack's late strike for a dubious offside here, Liverpool would have pipped Derby and Leeds to the honours on goal average.

3. Liverpool 3 Arsenal 1 11 August 1979

The champions claimed the Charity Shield against the FA Cup holders, thanks in part to a classic goal from Terry McDermott created by the Jedi-like telepathic skills of Kenny Dalglish. McDermott and Dalglish got Liverpool's other goals between them.

4. Arsenal 0 Liverpool 2 10 September 1983

Michael Robinson's backheel to set up Dalglish's magical left-foot curler for the second goal was the highlight of a breathtaking display of pass-and-move at its finest. "They seem to find angles other teams don't appreciate," announced John Motson. "You can count the passes and appreciate them all."

5. Liverpool 2 Arsenal 0 17 August 1985

Kenny Dalglish began his managerial career in August 1985 with an impressive defeat of Don Howe's Arsenal at Anfield. Ronnie Whelan headed the Reds into a first-half lead, before Dalglish himself set up Steve Nicol to head home the second.

6. Arsenal 1 Liverpool 2 15 August 1987
The start of a classic era as Liverpool, shimmering in silver on a scorching afternoon in N5, face up to life without Ian Rush by unveiling a formidable new striking force of Barnes, Beardsley and Aldridge. It's the last of this trio who scores the first after eight minutes, with Steve Nicol sealing the points two minutes from time.

7. Liverpool 2 Arsenal 0 16 January 1988
This was the symphony screened live across the globe with Michel Platini in the stands, purring at a masterpiece performance from the Reds. McMahon's bionic persistence set up the first for John Aldridge before the break; Peter Beardsley's delightful chip over John Lukic provided the second.

8. Liverpool 2 Arsenal 1 26 November 1989
Revenge of sorts for 26 May 1989 as the Reds defeat George Graham's team in a live Sunday afternoon game, Barnes charmed the perfect free kick into the top left-hand corner of John Lukic's goal. Cue Brian Moore: "Barnes... brilliant!"

9. Arsenal 1 Liverpool 2 24 March 1997
Best remembered for Robbie Fowler's moment of sportsmanship, this Monday night classic saw Stan Collymore put the Reds in front on 50 minutes before Jason McAteer turned in Fowler's saved penalty. Ian Wright pulled one back for Arsenal 12 minutes from time to set up a nail-biting finale.

10. Liverpool 4 Arsenal 0 23 December 2000
Liverpool's most comprehensive defeat of the Gunners came just two days before Christmas. Goals from Steven Gerrard, Michael Owen, Nick Barmby and substitute Robbie Fowler wrapped up the three points.

> BARNES CHARMED THE PERFECT FREE KICK INTO THE TOP LEFT-HAND CORNER. "BARNES...BRILLIANT!"

11. Liverpool 2 Arsenal 1 28 November 2004
Neil Mellor might never score a better or more important goal than this last-minute winner in front of the Kop. Xabi Alonso had put the Reds in front following a sublime ball from Gerrard, but Patrick Vieira equalised against the run of play on 57 minutes before Mellor's last-gasp heroics.

11. SHANKLY'S FIRST MATCH

Slater

Wheeler   White   Moran

Morris   Campbell   Jones   Melia   A'Court

Hunt   Hickson

The start of an era sees Shankly's first match in charge end in a 0-4 Division Two defeat to Cardiff City on 19 December 1959.

SPORT STARS WHO SUPPORT LIVERPOOL

The winners who cheer for English football's perennial winners

1. **Sven-Goran Eriksson** football manager
2. **Angus Fraser** cricketer
3. **Laura Davies** golfer
4. **Ceri Sweeney** rugby union player
5. **Graeme Smith** cricketer
6. **Steve Smith** former athlete
7. **Jermaine Pennant** footballer
8. **Paul Hodgkinson** boxer
9. **Darren Clarke** golfer
10. **Bobby Goulding** rugby league player
11. **Rio Ferdinand** footballer

STARS AND THEIR FOOTWEAR

The boots you coveted as a kid

1. **Kenny Dalglish** Puma
2. **Ian Rush** Nike
3. **Michael Owen** Umbro
4. **Robbie Fowler** Nike
5. **John Barnes** Diadora
6. **Terry McDermott** Adidas
7. **Steve McManaman** Umbro
8. **John Aldridge** Nike
9. **Steve McMahon** Hi-Tec
10. **Patrik Berger** Nike
11. **Ray Kennedy** Adidas

SUPREME SKIPPERS

11 inspirational Reds leaders

1. **Andrew Hannah** 1892-95
2. **Alex Raisbeck** 1899-1909
3. **Ephraim Longworth** 1912-20
4. **Billy Liddell** 1955-58
5. **Ron Yeats** 1961-70
6. **Tommy Smith** 1970-73
7. **Emlyn Hughes** 1973-79
8. **Phil Thompson** 1979-82
9. **Graeme Souness** 1982-84
10. **Alan Hansen** 1985-90
11. **Sami Hyypia** 2001-03

TEAMS THAT HAVE KNOCKED LIVERPOOL OUT OF EUROPE

Some of Europe's finest have dumped the Reds out of international competition

1. **Ajax** 7-3, European Cup, 1966/67
2. **Ferencvaros** 2-0, Inter-Cities Fairs Cup, 1967/68; 1-1, away goals, Cup Winners' Cup, 1974/75
3. **Leeds United** 1-0, Inter-Cities Fairs Cup, 1970/71
4. **Red Star Belgrade** 4-2, European Cup, 1973/74
5. **Widzew Lodz** 4-3, European Cup, 1982/83
6. **Genoa 1893** 4-1, UEFA Cup, 1991/92
7. **Spartak Moscow** 6-2, Cup Winners' Cup, 1992/93
8. **Brondby** 1-0, UEFA Cup, 1995/96
9. **Bayer Leverkusen** 4-3, Champions League, 2001/02
10. **Celta Vigo** 4-1, UEFA Cup, 1998/99
11. **Marseille** 3-2, UEFA Cup, 2003/04

TESTIMONIALS

11 faithful servants rewarded with a high-scoring. big benefit night at Anfield…

1. **Roger Hunt** 1972, v England XI, 8-6
2. **Bill Shankly** 1975, v Don Revie Select XI, 6-2
3. **Tommy Smith** 1977, v Bobby Charlton XI, 9-9
4. **Ray Clemence** 1980, v Anderlecht, 6-8
5. **Alan Hansen** 1988, v England XI, 3-2
6. **Kenny Dalglish** 1990, v Real Sociedad, 3-1
7. **Ray Kennedy** 1991, v Arsenal, 3-1
8. **Steve Nicol** 1993, v Terry Venables' Great Britain XI, 1-2
9. **Ian Rush** 1994, v Celtic, 6-0
10. **Jan Molby** 1996, v PSV Eindhoven, 2-3
11. **Ronnie Moran** 2000, v Celtic, 4-1

THIS IS ANFIELD

Extraordinary chapters in the illustrious history of football's most-storied stadium

1. The first stand, built in 1886 on Kemlyn Road, cost £64.

2. The suggestion to name the main terrace the Spion Kop came from local newspaper journalist Ernest Edwards.

3. In 1921, King George V and Queen Mary attended the ground to watch an FA Cup semi-final between Cardiff City and Wolves.

4. Between the wars, the ground played host to exhibition tennis matches and the finish of the Liverpool Civic Marathon.

5. In 1928, a mast from one of the first iron ships, the *Great Eastern*, was hauled up Everton Valley by a team of horses and erected next to the Kop as a flagpole.

6. Nel Tarleton fought Freddie Miller for the world featherweight title here in 1934.

7. In 1944, world heavyweight boxing champion Joe Louis signed professional forms for Liverpool at Anfield in a publicity stunt.

8. In 1967, as Liverpool played an FA Cup tie in front of 64,851 fans at Goodison Park, another 40,149 watched on a giant screen at Anfield.

9. Evangelist Billy Graham brought his Mission England tour to Anfield in July 1984.

10. In the 1980s, Anfield was home to a cat called Moglet.

11. The last "goal" in front of the Kop was scored by a fan, John Garner, who ran on the pitch after the 1-0 defeat by Norwich City in 1994 and blasted a ball into the net.

IN THE 1980S, ANFIELD WAS HOME TO A CAT CALLED MOGLET

TOP EUROPEAN GOALSCORERS

Liverpool's most prolific marksmen in the continental arena

1. **Michael Owen** 22
2. **Ian Rush** 20
3. **Roger Hunt** 17
4. **Terry McDermott** 15
5. **Jimmy Case** 13
   Emile Heskey 13
7. **Robbie Fowler** 12
   Kevin Keegan 12
   Ray Kennedy 12
10. **Kenny Dalglish** 11
    Steve Heighway 11
    Chris Lawler 11
    Phil Neal 11

TOP FA CUP SCORERS

Rushie leads the way in the pantheon of great Liverpool cup scorers

1. **Ian Rush** 39
2. **Roger Hunt** 18
3. **John Barnes** 16
   Harry Chambers 16
5. **Kevin Keegan** 14
6. **Kenny Dalglish** 13
   Billy Liddell 13
8. **Robbie Fowler** 12
   Ian St John 12
   Jack Balmer 12
11. **Peter Beardsley** 11
    Bill Lacey 11

TOP SCORERS IN A LEAGUE SEASON

And nobody's scored more than Sir Roger in one season for the Reds

1. **Roger Hunt** 41 in 1961/62
2. **Gordon Hodgson** 36 in 1930/31
3. **Ian Rush** 32 in 1983/84
4. **Roger Hunt** 31 in 1963/64
   Sam Raybould 31 in 1902/03
6. **Ian Rush** 30 in 1986/87
   Roger Hunt 30 in 1965/66
   Billy Liddell 30 in 1954/55
   Gordon Hodgson 30 in 1928/29
10. **Michael Owen** 28 in 2001/02
    Robbie Fowler 28 in 1995/96

TRADEMARKS

"They'll all be trying that in the playground tomorrow…"

1. The John Barnes shimmy
2. The Alan Hansen stride
3. The Joey Jones fist-clench
4. The Mark Lawrenson slide-tackle
5. The Kenny Dalglish shield
6. The Djibril Cisse somersault
7. The Jamie Redknapp curler
8. The Patrik Berger thunderbolt
9. The John Arne Riise shirt-raise
10. The John Aldridge shuffle
11. The Emile Heskey scratch

UNFORGETTABLE CLASHES WITH MANCHESTER UNITED

There's nothing better than beating our rivals or staging a sensational comeback

1. Liverpool 7 Manchester United 1 1895
United were still known as Newton Heath in October 1895 when Liverpool pulled off their biggest-ever victory over the Mancunians, a 7-1 rout in Division Two. Frank Becton, Thomas Bradshaw, Fred Geary all scored two and Jimmy Ross rounded off the romp.

2. Liverpool 3 Manchester United 0 1964
En route to their first championship in 17 years, the Reds comprehensively defeated United, and the man who put two of the goals past Harry Gregg was a Mancunian, striker Alf Arrowsmith. Ian Callaghan scored the first goal after six minutes.

3. Liverpool 2 Manchester United 2 1979
The Reds might have lost the replay of this FA Cup semi-final, but the first game will be remembered ever more for a supreme first-half finish from Dalglish after dancing through Buchan, McIlroy and Bailey, and Alan Hansen uncharacteristically sprinting the length of the Maine Road pitch after netting a late equaliser.

4. Manchester United 1 Liverpool 2 1990
Sublime in silver, John Barnes tormented United on a Sunday afternoon in March 1990, converting a penalty on 15 minutes and making it two in the second half. Oh, and Ronnie Whelan scored the most spectacular own goal of all-time, a beautiful arcing lob over the head of the helpless Grobbelaar

5. Liverpool 2 Manchester United 0 1992
The Mancs seemed to have their first title in 25 years all wrapped up, but their quest faltered as spring dawned and Leeds overtook them. They had to win at Anfield to stay in the race, but on a bright Sunday, Ian Rush, scoring his first-ever goal against

United, and Mark Walters crushed their dreams as *Always Look On The Bright Side Of Life* rang round Anfield and Lee Chapman celebrated on his sofa.

6. Liverpool 3 Manchester United 3 1994
One of the most dramatic comebacks in Anfield history. United raced into a 3-0 lead in under half an hour through Bruce, Giggs and Irwin, but Nigel Clough pulled two back before the break. Neil Ruddock's late bullet header set the flares on the Kop alight, even if the concussed Razor couldn't quite comprehend what was going on.

7. Liverpool 2 Manchester United 0 1995
The highlight on a freezing, but satisfying December afternoon at Anfield was undoubtedly Robbie Fowler's sweet free kick just on half-time, taking the shortest of step-ups and manoeuvring the ball perfectly around United's grey-clad wall. Robbie wrapped up the points with a second three minutes from the end.

8. Liverpool 2 Manchester United 2 1999
History almost repeated itself as the Reds fell two goals behind to Yorke and Irwin. But a Jamie Redknapp penalty set up a pulsating finale, climaxed by Paul Ince's last-minute equaliser in front of the Kop against his former team-mates.

9. Liverpool 2 Manchester United 0 2001
Steven Gerrard's first-half rocket put the Reds on the road to the second half of a Premiership double against Fergie's men in 2000/01, celebrated with a belly flop. Robbie Fowler ruined Fabien Barthez's day with a fierce shot just before half-time, and even Danny Murphy's sending off couldn't dampen the celebrations.

10. Liverpool 3 Manchester United 1 2001
The Kop pay homage to Houllier, recuperating after his heart op. The team do likewise with a relentless performance, crowned by an unstoppable John Arne Riise free kick from 28 yards, sandwiched by two strikes from Owen.

11. Manchester United 0 Liverpool 1 2004
Danny Murphy had an extraordinary record against United, having already scored the winner in two 1-0 victories at Old Trafford. In April 2004 he made it three from the spot after Gary Neville had given away a penalty on 63 minutes. United threw the kitchen sink at Liverpool, but couldn't penetrate the Reds' defence.

UNFORGETTABLE TELEVISION COMMENTARIES

The classic words of Coleman and co that are etched in every fan's memory

1. "There's a man being arrested, but he doesn't care. Ee-aye-addio, we scored a goal! Six policemen and he's still waving his rattle!"
Kenneth Wolstenholme on a one-man pitch invasion during the 1965 FA Cup final

2. "Goals pay the rent, and Keegan does his share... Liverpool showing their party pieces, yes! Keegan's second and Newcastle were undressed, they were absolutely stripped naked... Keegan 2 Heighway 1, Liverpool 3 Newcastle none!"
David Coleman delights in Newcastle's demise in the FA Cup final, 1974

3. "That's nice, that's McDermott, and that's a goal..."
"Oh, and what a delighted scorer, it's Tommy Smith! Look at it again..."
"And with such simplicity, surely the European Cup has been won!"
Barry Davies describes Liverpool's three goals in the European Cup final against Borussia Moenchengladbach, 1977

4. "And Johnson, the ball into acres of empty space for Heighway and Heighway, a brilliant cross... McDermott it was who finished it off, and what a brilliant goal! Tottenham... in remnants!"
Gerald Sinstadt as Liverpool complete the 7-0 rout of Spurs in 1978

5. "Still no goals, and here's Dalglish, over his head and De Cubber was there, but so is Sowness [sic] there, will he get a shot in? Now, Dalglish across the face of the goal... it's there, Dalglish! Just look at those Liverpool players... brilliant scenes of joy! The little chip by Dalglish and the magic sight of that ball in the back of the Bruges net!"
Brian Moore gets everything but Souey's name right in the 1978 European Cup final

6. "Dalglish, beautiful turn, oh and on for Rush, what a perfect through ball, and what a brilliant goal! Ian Rush celebrates the goal, but Kenny Dalglish the creator supreme! The Kop celebrates, Dalglish and Rush do it again."
Alan Parry sums up a classic from a legendary partnership against Watford, 1982

7. "Grobbelaar, antics on the line... Missed it! Missed it! So Liverpool are 3-2 up... If Alan Kennedy scores, it's all over and Liverpool have won... Liverpool are European champions! What joy! A penalty kick leaves Rome distraught and Merseyside jubilant."
Brian Moore on the spot for the 1984 European Cup final penalty shoot-out

8. "Molby, oh I say, his vision there was lovely. Here's Whelan. He's got Dalglish... and

Rush is on the far side. Is this three? It is!"
John Motson on the mic as the Reds secure the Double, 1986

9. "Beardsley! That's a lovely goal, that's a lovely goal! Oh, and he even gets a kiss for it, from a man incidentally wearing a blue striped shirt!"
Barry Davies on Peter Beardsley's goal against Everton, 1987

10. "Barnes, Rush, Barnes. Still John Barnes… Collymore closing in! Liverpool lead in stoppage time! Kevin Keegan hangs his head, he's devastated!"
Martin Tyler on the last-gasp winner in the 4-3 victory over Newcastle, 1996

11. "Oh, that's Boy's Own stuff! It's been that kind of night and it's been wonderful"
Barry Davies on Robbie Fowler's finish against Alaves in the UEFA Cup final, 2001

UNSUNG HEROES

The Reds wouldn't have conquered England and Europe without this lot

1. Stig Inge Bjornebye
The Norwegian defender struggled initially with the pace of the Premiership, but under Roy Evans something just clicked, and his crosses from wing-back became integral to the team's 5-3-2 system, earning him a place in the PFA team of 1996/97.

2. Peter Cormack
The Scottish midfielder made 178 appearances for Liverpool, but never really received the recognition his talents deserved, being blessed with an impressive array of skills and tricks, and struck up an impressive rapport with Kevin Keegan.

3. Brian Hall
Little Bamber stood just 5ft 6in but that didn't prevent him from being a consistent performer on the right of midfield in the early 1970s. The BSc made 222 appearances in the red shirt, making tireless runs and dispatching crosses, and had a terrier-like nature that made life tricky for opponents.

4. Gary Gillespie
The classy, commanding Scottish defender arrived from Coventry City in 1983 but had to wait patiently behind Hansen and Lawrenson for the chance of regular first-team football. Eventually he got it, clocking up 214 appearances, memorably netting an improbable hat-trick against Birmingham City in 1986.

5. Didi Hamann

Liverpool's midfield insurance man under Gerard Houllier and Rafael Benitez, the German has been effortlessly tidying up in front of defence for six seasons. His long-range shooting is not the most accurate but it's unstoppable when on target, earning him goal of the season for his piledriver against Portsmouth in 2004.

6. Stephane Henchoz

The Swiss defender struck up a magnificent relationship with Sami Hyypia but never earned the same praise. A tireless, battling performer, he played 205 matches for Liverpool, although infamously he never managed to get on the score sheet.

7. Sammy Lee

He might have been fat, he might have been round and yes, he did bounce on the ground, but the Scouse midfielder was one of England's most consistent midfielders, marking Bayern Munich captain Paul Breitner out of the 1981 European Cup semi.

8. Danny Murphy

The talented midfielder did earn England recognition during his seven seasons at Liverpool, but too many erratic performances overshadowed his achievements. His feat of scoring the winner against Manchester United on three separate occasions is undeniably impressive.

9. Nigel Spackman

The powerful midfielder never carved out a regular first-team role after joining in 1987, but he became a hero in his 66 appearances. Wore an appalling headband in the 1988 FA Cup final after clashing heads with Gary Gillespie in training.

10. Michael Thomas

He scored the goal that every Liverpool supporter wants to forget, but after moving to Anfield in a shock move in 1991, the midfielder netted a spectacular volleyed goal to remember in the club's 2-0 defeat of Sunderland in the 1992 FA Cup final. He made 163 appearances in seven seasons at the club.

11. Ronnie Whelan

Despite some stunning goals in big games, the intelligent Irish midfielder is perhaps the club's most underrated footballer of all, holding things together in the engine room while other players caught the eye. He won 12 major honours in his time at Anfield, including six league championships.

UNUSUAL COMPETITIONS

"The Screen Sport Super what…?"

1. European Super Cup

Liverpool have competed four times for the Super Cup, the first pitting Kevin Keegan and his new club Hamburg against his old team. The Reds ran out 7-1 winners on aggregate, sealing the second leg 6-0 thanks to a hat-trick from Terry McDermott in front of a gleeful Kop chanting, "We all agree, Dalglish is better than Keegan!" The following year, Liverpool lost the trophy 4-3 on aggregate, including a bizarre second leg at an Anfield shrouded in fog. An encounter with Dynamo Tbilisi in 1981 never took place, and the Reds lost a one-off match against Juventus 2-0 in Turin in 1985. The UEFA Cup success of 2001 earned them another shot, staged in Monaco as the prelude to the European season, and the Reds won their second Super Cup, defeating Bayern Munich 3-2 with goals from Riise, Heskey and Owen.

2. World Club Championship

The Reds might well be the greatest team the world has ever seen, but both the club's bouts for the world heavyweight title ended in failure. In 1981, as European Cup holders, Liverpool travelled to Japan to face South American champions Flamengo of Brazil, Zico and all. The Reds came off second best, losing 3-0 to goals from Nunes (2) and Adilio. Three years later, it was back to Tokyo as thousands of bleary-eyed Reds fans tuned into ITV's live coverage at 3am, having sat through Joan Collins romp *The Bitch* beforehand. But Liverpool never recovered from José Alberto Percudani's early goal for Independiente of Argentina, and lost 1-0.

3. Screen Sport Super Cup

The Football League devised this tournament as a form of consolation for the six English clubs banned from Europe in 1985/86 in the wake of the Heysel tragedy. Dogged by a byzantine format and dismal crowds, it was never repeated but Liverpool became its first and only winners, beating Everton 7-2 on aggregate in a final held over to the following season. Five of the goals came from Ian Rush.

4. Football League Centenary Festival

Masterminded by Jimmy Hill, the Centenary Festival remains the most surreal football tournament ever. Sixteen clubs gathered at a deserted Wembley in April 1988 to celebrate the Football League's 100th birthday with a two-day knockout tournament of 20-minute matches, causing the entire league programme to be postponed. Liverpool's participation began at 10.30am on the Saturday and ended shortly after, their 0-0 draw with Newcastle settled by a sudden-death shoot-out in which Steve McMahon missed and Neil McDonald scored. And that was it.

5. Football League Centenary Trophy

But the festivities continued in the autumn of 1988, when the top eight teams from the previous season participated in the little-prized Centenary Trophy. The Reds knocked out Nottingham Forest 4-1 in the first round, only to lose 2-1 to Arsenal at Highbury in the semi-finals.

6. The Makita International

Little more than a pre-season kickabout, albeit one played underneath the twin towers of Wembley in the summer of 1989. Barnes and Aldridge helped dispatch Dynamo Kiev 2-0 on day one, but the Reds lost 1-0 to Arsenal in the final.

7. Guinness Soccer Six

Liverpool have always been reluctant to take part in this kind of thing, but in 1990 the Reds participated in this annual indoor tournament at Manchester's G-Mex Centre for the first and only time. Liverpool's squad boasted only three first-teamers – Peter Beardsley, Jan Molby and Ronnie Rosenthal – and the goalkeeper – Carl Muggleton – was on loan from Leicester. The Reds beat Everton and drew with Aston Villa in the group matches to reach the final against Luton Town. But the Hatters were more used to the artificial pitch and artificial surroundings, and routed Liverpool 4-0.

8. Dubai Super Cup

In December 1986 the Reds travelled to the Far East to take part in what is invariably described as a "lucrative friendly", in this case a showdown between the English and Scottish champions. Liverpool's goal in a 1-1 draw with Celtic came from Alan Hansen, before the Reds ran out 4-2 winners on penalties. They returned in April 1989, again to face Celtic, and the scoreline was 1-1 once more, John Aldridge hitting the net, although this time the Bhoys triumphed in the shoot-out.

9. Caltex Cup

Remember the Caltex Cup? No, not many people do. In May 1991, having just lost the league title to Arsenal, the Reds travelled to Singapore to face the Gunners again in an exhibition match. Despite Ian Rush's 52nd minute goal, Liverpool came off second best to George Graham's team once more, losing on penalties after a 1-1 draw in front of 45,000 spectators.

10. Coppa Pirelli

Liverpool did battle for the Coppa Pirelli in a pre-season match against Inter Milan in 1998, as part of the deal that brought Paul Ince to Anfield. In front of 44,146 fans, the Reds beat the Italian giants 2-1, thanks to goals from Steve Harkness and Ince himself.

11. Football League 100th Championship Challenge

In 1999, the Reds once again participated in a Football League centenary knees-up, this time to mark the 100th season of the competition they won a record 18 times before the advent of the Premiership. They took on Division One reigning champions Sunderland at the Stadium Of Light, running out 3-2 winners with strikes from Robbie Fowler, Jamie Redknapp and Paul Ince.

VINTAGE KENNY DALGLISH MOMENTS

Read. Absorb. Worship

1. The beautiful chest and volley to win the league at Stamford Bridge in 1986
2. The delicious left-footed curler against Arsenal at Highbury in 1983
3. The backheel to set up Phil Neal against Aberdeen in 1980
4. The turn, dribble and spectacular volley at Derby County in 1979
5. The run, twist and blast in the 1979 Charity Shield against Arsenal
6. The impudent backflick from two yards out at Aston Villa in 1978
7. The blistering swerving right-footer after 15 seconds at Everton in 1985
8. The pivot and shot against West Ham in the 1981 League Cup final replay
9. The dribble and angled shot in a hat-trick against Manchester City in 1982
10. The slot past Paul Bradshaw after a three-man move against Wolves in 1979
11. The wriggle through the Manchester United defence in the 1979 FA Cup semi

WELSH REDS

11 Liverpool legends who hailed from the land of song

1. **Joey Jones** Llandudno
2. **Lee Jones** Wrexham
3. **Paul Jones** Chirk
4. **Ray Lambert** Bagillt
5. **Maurice Parry** Trefonen
6. **Ernest Peake** Aberystwyth
7. **Tony Rowley** Porthcawl
8. **Ian Rush** St Asaph
9. **Dean Saunders** Swansea
10. **Cyril Sidlow** Colwyn Bay
11. **John Toshack** Cardiff

WE'RE PLAYING WHO, BOSS?

11 of the most prestigious, most memorable, and just plain weird games

1. **St Louis Catholic Youth Council All Stars 1 Liverpool 1** tour match 1964
2. **San Franciscan Select 0 Liverpool 14** tour match 1964
3. **Saudi Arabia 1 Liverpool 1** friendly 1978
4. **Israel 1 Liverpool 4** friendly 1984
5. **Liverpool 5 Tottenham 2** Royal Swazi Sun Challenge 1984
6. **Celtic 0 Liverpool 4** Hillsborough fundraiser 1989
7. **Liverpool 2 Aston Villa 1** Nelson Mandela Soccer Festival 1994
8. **Liverpool 2 Leeds United 0** Carlsberg Belfast Challenge Trophy 1998
9. **Liverpool 2 AC Milan 1** Real Madrid Centenary Tournament 2002
10. **Hong Kong XI 0 Liverpool 6** tour match 2003
11. **Liverpool 2 Roma 1** USA Champions world Series 2004

THE WIZARD OF OZ

11 extraordinary exploits of Craig Johnston

1. Nearly having his leg amputated

The incredible Aussie, who was actually born in South Africa, contracted a form of polio called osteomyelitis at the age of six. The doctors wanted to amputate his left leg but his mother refused, sending him to the US for specialist treatment. It was this incident, believes Johnston, that spurred him into…

2. Becoming a crap footballer

Not true. In fact, on his day he was an imaginative midfielder with the energy of a crate of Red Bull. But try telling him that. "I was crap," he says. "You have no idea how crap I was. Even when I was playing for Liverpool, I was the worst player in the best team in the world." During his first match for Middlesbrough as a trainee, Jack Charlton dropped a hint in his half-time team talk. "You can f*** off right now, you kangaroo. You're the worst player I've seen in my life." Johnston devised his own training regime, which involved dribbling round dustbins. Blindfolded. It eventually earned him a transfer to Liverpool, and five years later, he found himself…

3. Scoring in the FA Cup final

It was Johnston who put the Reds ahead against Everton in the 1986 FA Cup final. Dalglish had failed to make contact with Molby's pass, but Johnston was unmarked at the far post to make it 2-1. Two years later, Liverpool reached Wembley once more, and Johnston marked the occasion by…

4. Writing a Top Ten single

Craig devised The Anfield Rap, Liverpool's 1988 FA Cup final record which reached No. 3 in the charts. It was one of the last things he did as a Liverpool player, for a few weeks later he announced his intention to…

5. Retire from football at the age of 27

In 1988, at the end of Liverpool's 17th championship season, Skippy said he was quitting football to return to Australia and look after his sister who was seriously ill. Johnston was definitely a family man, although not many on Merseyside had been entirely happy a few years earlier when he decided to…

6. Christen his daughter Chelsea

But it had nothing to do with football, he protested, he just liked the name. He once photographed her standing in the European Cup, because by then he had…

7. Become an ace photographer

"I'd spent most of my wages on photographic equipment," he recalls. "That's my first love. I even had a studio in Liverpool. I was never made to be a footballer mentally. I preferred to hang around with the press photographers after games. The skills he learned as a photographer helped him get into television, where he would…

8. Devise a top-rated game show

In 1990, Johnston created *The Main Event* for Australia's 7 Network, which involved celebrities playing games on behalf of families watching at home. The format was sold all over the world, although the British version was not a success. But perhaps his greatest triumph as an entrepreneur came when he decided to…

9. Invent the perfect football boot (and help Australia lose the Rugby World Cup in the process)

Johnston developed the Predator boot, which features a network of rubber and carbon-fibre nodules which give the wearer more control and power. He poured £500,000 of his own money into the idea and was turned down by Nike and Reebok before Adidas bought it on Franz Beckenbauer's recommendation. Adapted for rugby, and worn by Jonny Wilkinson when he scored the decisive kick for England in the 2003 World Cup final. But there was no stopping Johnston now, he'd had the idea to…

10. Produce a mini-bar security system

Bored in his hotel room during a promotional tour for the Predator boot, Johnston found himself pondering the problem of guests taking booze out of the mini-bar without paying. He devised a computerised sensor system called The Butler, which automatically registered items on the bill. It's sold more than 20,000 units. Johnston's passion for design was sparked at an early age, when he used to design kitchens for his mum. He was shortlisted as the Design Museum's designer of the year for the Predator, but Craig also had one eye on the silver screen, with his decision to…

11. Pitch a movie about Bill Shankly

In 2001, Johnston revealed he had been developing a film script about the Liverpool legend. "It's about him becoming disillusioned with football in Britain and moving to the United States." Don't bet against Craig picking up a few film awards.

CRAIG JOHNSTON'S PREDATOR BOOT HELPED ENGLAND WIN THE RUGBY WORLD CUP

WONDER GOALS

11 of the best. Probably.

1. Terry McDermott v Tottenham Hotspur 1978

A breathtaking, sweeping box-to-box move that developed out of a Spurs corner. The clearance reached Dalglish, who played it to Johnson, who turned and fired an immaculate 50-yard ball out wide to Heighway haring down the left. His cross was met perfectly by the head of Terry McDermott to make it 7-0. Majestic.

2. John Aldridge v Arsenal 1988

Not for Aldo's close-range finish, but for the amazing persistence of Steve McMahon in making it possible. Tony Adams thought he'd relieved the pressure by clearing the ball, only for McMahon to set off in pursuit and stop it, his momentum taking him off the pitch. He then dribbled past Adams to set up Beardsley to feed Aldridge.

3. Ian Rush v Watford 1982

A long ball from keeper Steve Sherwood is cleared by Phil Neal towards Dalglish, who spins seductively around his marker before playing the perfect curling through ball into the path of Rush, who fires it with his left foot into the corner of the net.

4. John Barnes v QPR 1987

The quintessential Barnes shimmy. He dispossesses Kevin Brock on the halfway line, dances through two defenders before coolly dispatching the ball under Seaman.

5. Kenny Dalglish v Bruges 1978

The delicate chip from the most acute of angles settled the 1978 European Cup final, after Graeme Souness had played a precise pass into the box for Dalglish to slot past Birger Jensen, then bound over the Wembley advertising hoardings in celebration.

6. Steve McManaman v Celtic 1997

Liverpool are trailing 2-1 with a minute to go in this UEFA Cup tie at Parkhead when Macca picks up the ball from David James on the right side of his own half. He plays a one-two with himself to push it past a Celtic defender, before weaving across the pitch and bending the ball with his left foot into the net from the edge of the box.

7. Steven Gerrard v Olympiakos 2004

Liverpool are just four minutes from exiting the Champions League at the group stage, when Steve Finnan swings in a ball to substitute Neil Mellor, who flicks it down across the edge of the box for Gerrard to blast unerringly in.

8. Robbie Fowler v Aston Villa 1996
The finest of the 171 goals Robbie Fowler scored for Liverpool, as he leaves Steve Staunton for dead with a backheeled flick, takes one touch and pulls the trigger to beat Villa keeper Mark Bosnich with a swerving shot in a 3-0 victory at Anfield.

9. Kevin Keegan v Newcastle United 1974
Seven players in all and a dozen passes were involved in the build-up to Liverpool's third goal in the 1974 FA Cup final. It started with Clemence, before Tommy Smith, Brian Hall and Steve Heighway put on their "party pieces", toying with the Magpies's defence, Smith dispatching the cross for Keegan to turn into an empty net.

10. Jimmy Case v Manchester United 1977
The 1977 FA Cup final defeat ended dreams of the Treble, but not before Case had scored a classic. Joey Jones floated in a ball from the left, Case picked it up on the edge of the box, took two touches as he spun and blasted it past Alex Stepney.

11. Ray Kennedy v Bristol City 1980
McDermott drives a 40-yard crossfield ball to Dalglish on the edge of the box. He controls it on his chest and plays it right to David Johnson, who chips it up for the late-arriving Kennedy to control and volley it into the top left hand corner.

WORLDWIDE REDS

Our lads have come from all over the place

1. **Pegguy Arphexad** Abymes, Guadeloupe
2. **John Barnes** Kingston, Jamaica
3. **Titi Camara** Conakry, Guinea
4. **Avi Cohen** Tel Aviv, Israel
5. **Salif Diao** Kedogou Tallie, Senegal
6. **El-Hadji Diouf** Daqar, Senegal
7. **Brad Friedel** Lakewood, Ohio, USA
8. **Bruce Grobbelaar** Durban, South Africa
9. **Ronnie Rosenthal** Haifa, Israel
10. **Rigobert Song** Nkenlicock, Cameroon
11. **Abel Xavier** Namula, Mozambique

X FILES

Totally random trivia

1. *Through The Wind and the Rain* is the longest-running Liverpool fanzine. *When Sunday Comes* has the honour of being the first.

2. After playing a record-breaking 843 games for the Reds, Ian Callaghan bought and ran a pub in Rufford, Lancashire.

3. From 1980 to 1984, Liverpool went 25 rounds in the League and Milk Cup without losing a game.

4. When Kevin Keegan and Billy Bremner were sent off for fighting in the 1974 Charity Shield, both were banned for 11 games – three for the fight, eight for ripping off their shirts in disgust.

5. Former Reds captain Emlyn Hughes appeared on a cassette given away in the 1980s, singing the praises of a homebrew kit.

6. *The Times* once reported that Liverpool were to sign a player who didn't exist. Gerard Houllier's alleged target, the £3.5 million-rated French under-21 international Didier Baptiste was a character in a TV soap opera.

7. Liverpool benefited from one of the craziest own goals ever when Leeds keeper Gary Sprake changed his mind halfway through throwing out the ball and threw the ball straight into his own net. Ever-sympathetic, at half time, the Liverpool DJ played *Careless Hands* by Des O'Connor.

8. Striker George Allan so upset legendary keeper William 'Fatty' Foulke that the Chelsea No 1 picked him up, and stuck his head in the mud.

9. In the Liverpool museum at Anfield, you'll find one of Craig Johnston's old surfboards.

10. The second half of a match between Liverpool and Huddersfield in 1948 started without a referee. A whistle blew in the crowd and the players, assuming it was the referee's, kicked off.

11. Liverpool's lowest ever league attendance was just 1,000 – for a match against Loughborough Town in 1895.